Copyright © 2008 David F. Jones

Published by CPO Publishing
101 Forrest Crossing Boulevard
Suite 100
Franklin, Tennessee 37064

Library of Congress Cataloging-in-Publication Data

Jones, David F.
  Surviving and thriving after losing your job : how this could be the best thing that's ever happened to you / David F. Jones.
      p. cm. -- (Your first 30 days)
  Includes bibliographical references.
  ISBN 978-1-59186-600-8 (trade paper : alk. paper)
  1. Unemployed--Psychology. 2. Career development. 3. Job hunting. I. Title. II. Series.

  HD5708.J66 2008
  650.14--dc22

2008027681

First Printing 2008
Printed in the United States of America
10 9 8 7 6 5 4 3 2 1

Production: Publication Services, Inc.
Cover Design: Marc Pewitt

SURVIVING and THRIVING after

LOSING YOUR

JOB

HOW THIS COULD BE
THE BEST THING THAT'S
EVER HAPPENED TO YOU

DAVID F. JONES

CPO
PUBLISHING
Franklin, Tennessee

CONTENTS

ACKNOWLEDGMENTS

My life has been an incredible blessing and journey. This book is dedicated to those who brought, and continue to bring, immense love and joy to my life: my wife Tanya, who has been my rock for the last thirty-one years and the wind beneath our family's wings; my son Josh and my daughter Kim, whom we are tremendously proud of and thankful for; and my father, L. D. Jones, who has been an inspiration for me: he is as much a friend as a father.

During my corporate career, I've had the privilege of working for four great bosses: Ken Horton, David Gosselin, Gilmer Abel, and Dan Martin. I appreciate the things each of you taught me and the chance you took to give me an opportunity to prove myself when others might have doubted.

I appreciate the opportunity John Zurcher and Mark Hereth, my consulting colleagues, gave me when I started my new career. It's been both a pleasure and a learning experience to work with both of you.

The support, friendship, and encouragement of many

friends over the years have been invaluable to me. Dr. John Bright Cage, we've laughed together and cried together over the last thirty years, and I look forward to many more Monday morning breakfasts with you at Cracker Barrel. To the Outlaw Gang—Coleman Boyd, Doug Lackey, and Jim Lackey: we've ridden our Harleys tens of thousands of miles together over the years, and I look forward to more road miles and adventures with you in the years to come.

Thanks to Roger Waynick, Doug Norfleet, and the great folks at CPO Publishing for helping make my dream of writing a book come true.

And, finally—Lord, I am so very blessed and grateful.

Dare to be a Daniel,
Dare to stand alone;
Dare to have a purpose,
Dare to make it known.

PHILIP PAUL BLISS, AMERICAN HYMN WRITER

You're fired!" Donald Trump and *The Apprentice* have made these two words famous. Each week, a couple of aspiring apprentices from the week's losing team are brought into the board room by the team's project manager. The three of them have a couple of pressure-packed minutes to answer Trump's pointed questions and convince him to fire one of the other apprentices. Trump listens to their arguments and accusations, points his finger at one of them, and utters those two dreaded words: "You're fired." The fired apprentice is promptly escorted from the boardroom to an awaiting taxi to be driven away along with dreams of winning the show and working for Trump. It's an interesting so-called reality show. All the contestants on the show have temporarily left good jobs or businesses to be on the show, knowing that if they didn't win, they could return to their old jobs or even use the television exposure to find better ones.

"You're fired" is being heard more and more across America each day by hundreds of employees. I doubt bosses always use those words, but the end result is the same. For every employee hearing those dreaded words, it's not a reality show—it's a reality nightmare. Unlike the "apprentices," employees who are being terminated don't have other jobs to go back to. If you're reading this, it means you've probably lost your job. Join the club. This book is written to help you transition from "you're fired" to "you're hired."

I always dreamed about writing a book someday. I didn't think, however, it would be the result of getting fired in the middle of a very successful corporate career. Writing a book was one of the goals on the "107 List" I wrote back in my early thirties, over twenty years ago. I had read a newspaper article on Lou Holtz, who at that time was head football coach at Notre Dame University, in which he talked about something he called his "107 List." It was a list he had written when he had just been hired as an assistant coach at the University of South Carolina, at the age of twenty-eight. At the time, his wife was pregnant with their third child and he had just overextended himself to buy a new house. One month later, the head coach who had just hired him resigned, and Holtz found himself unemployed and questioning whether or not he was in the right profession. He was downcast and unmotivated, so his wife gave him a book—*The Magic of Thinking Big,* by David Schwartz—to help lift his spirits. The book advised that he write down all the goals he wished to achieve during his life. Lou did what the book suggested, and his final list included financial-, spiritual-, professional-, family-, and leisure-related goals. It helped turn Holtz's life around, and it certainly seemed like a good idea to me. Having always been a goal-setter, I didn't need much inspiration to start my own 107 List, which has grown over the years to more than two hundred goals. In addition to writing a book, another goal I put on my list that day was starting my own company. I had spent my entire career in corporate America, but imagined it would be fun to work for myself—to be my own boss and to see if I could successfully start and grow my own business. When I developed my original 107 List, I never could have guessed that seemingly separate goals of writing a book and starting my own business would one day be linked. As it turned out, they were inextricably linked.

People lose their jobs for a myriad of reasons. Some people lose their jobs because of incompetence, insubordination, stealing, and other personal faults. I don't have a lot of empathy for these people, because they create their own problems and must live with the consequences. Nevertheless, this book can help those individuals if they are willing to own up to their shortcomings or mistakes and start fresh.

This book is targeted at those individuals—whether blue-collar workers, professionals, or executives—who lose their jobs for no fault of their own. Each day in America, hundreds of employees are terminated because of corporate mergers, acquisitions, downsizing, and realignments. Like you, most of these employees had poured their hearts and souls into the companies that employed them. Many of these employees can tell you about the personal sacrifices they made for their companies, working late nights and long weekends, missing birthdays, disrupting or even canceling vacations. Why did they make these sacrifices? Maybe they believed it was expected, or maybe they did it to simply help strengthen their companies out of a strong sense of commitment and loyalty—only to be rewarded by their bosses unexpectedly walking into their offices one day to tell them their jobs were being eliminated and to ask them to pack up their personal belongings, turn in their company keys and credit cards, and exit the premises.

This isn't a new phenomenon. It's been happening in

America for the better part of two decades, and few companies are immune to it. It will probably continue indefinitely as more and more businesses struggle to compete in today's global economy. Companies must be especially competitive to survive today, and employee salaries are often one of the largest, if not the largest, expenses, and thus a prime target for cost reductions. But knowing you can lose your job at any moment doesn't make it any less painful when the axe actually falls. When you're fired, you must face reality and move on with your life and your career.

I hope this book helps you to move on to bigger and better things in your life. I've divided it into two parts. Part One explores how and why corporate America is changing and discusses how to deal with the emotional ups and downs you experience after being terminated. It also explores ways to develop a support group to help you weather the emotional and physiological storm. Part Two of the book discusses coping with change, discovering your life's purpose, developing a game plan for finding a new job or career, marketing yourself, and starting over. I've shared my own experiences during the time that I lost my job, as well as the experiences of several others who also lost theirs. My goal in writing this book isn't just to help you successfully transition from being terminated to finding *a* job. I want you to use your momentary job or career "time-out" to think broadly and holistically about your next job or career. Unshackled by your past, you have an opportunity to reinvent yourself and create an exciting and fulfilling job, career, and life. Do you have the courage to do so?

PART ONE

SURVIVING THE STORM

CHAPTER ONE

Merry Christmas

A bend in the road is not the end of
the road ... unless you fail to make the turn.

AUTHOR UNKNOWN

For me, September 21, 2006, started off like any other day at the office. I was busy handling e-mails, returning phone calls, and reading reports. In the afternoon, my telephone rang. It was my boss, Dan Martin, senior vice president of operations and engineering. Dan said he needed to share something very confidential and asked me to close my office door, which, historically, wasn't a good sign. As I got out of my chair and walked over to close my door, I quickly recalled three other times Dan had called me and started his conversation the same way. Each of those times, our company, El Paso Corporation, was in the process of acquiring another company pipeline, which meant months of difficult merger and acquisition work—and inevitable changes. I knew we couldn't be acquiring another pipeline company: our debt was still too high from all the previous mergers, and we would be facing approval problems with the Federal Trade Commission as the largest natural gas transmission company in the United States. I was right—we weren't buying another company this time. He told me that El Paso had decided to sell one of its five pipeline companies to further reduce our corporate debt. The company to be sold was ANR Pipeline, one of the three I was responsible for managing as vice president of eastern operations. While he was talking, thoughts raced through my mind: Why sell one of our best assets, particularly after all the work we had gone through to merge it into our organization only five years ago? Who would the buyer be? How would we explain this to the other non–ANR Pipeline field employees, whom we had been telling that all the pipelines were core assets to El Paso? How would this affect ANR employees? How would this affect *my* job, since I managed this pipeline along with two others?

The sale had to be kept highly confidential, and only a few companies and investors would be approached to see whether they were interested in submitting sealed bids for the pipeline. Dan indicated that four or five El Paso officers were to go with the sale, one of them from operations—there was a possibility it could be me. It didn't hit me at that moment, but my world was about to radically change. He said the potential buyer would most likely need a senior management team to run ANR Pipeline, especially if it wasn't another pipeline company. From experience with previous mergers, I knew that if the buyer was another pipeline company, there was a good chance they would put their own management team into place, putting me out of a job. On the other hand, if the buyer didn't have any energy or pipeline experience, it could be a great opportunity for those going with ANR. The news from the call wasn't exactly what I had hoped to hear, but, as usual, I appreciated Dan's honesty and frankness. He promised to keep me posted when he knew more about the next steps—particularly how I might be affected. He told me he didn't want me to go with the sale and would do everything he could to try to keep me with El Paso, but he said he couldn't promise anything. I'd been through enough of these deals to know he couldn't make me any promises, and I didn't expect him to. But I appreciated hearing those words from him, and I knew he meant them. I told him I didn't want to leave El Paso at this juncture of my career, but I understood the dilemma he was facing, and I knew my job with El Paso was clearly at risk. I was only a few months from celebrating my thirtieth anniversary with El Paso. I couldn't help but wonder if I would be at the upcoming service award banquet.

The next few months, from October to December, were hectic because El Paso wanted to complete the transaction by year's end. A select few El Paso employees worked secretly to pull together an electronic data room, making presentations to prospective bidders and deciding which employees and company assets would go with the sale. I found out in late October that I definitely would be one of the officers going with the sale. It was a trying time for all of us working on the sale, but particularly for the few of us who knew we were going to be a part of it. We also had to keep working at our regular jobs, making company decisions about things we wouldn't be around to see come to fruition. It was very hard to keep my heart in my job, and I hated that I could not tell my subordinates what was going to happen to ANR Pipeline and me. In a few months, they would have a new boss, and I might, too—but I also didn't know who mine would be, provided the buyer offered me a job with their company.

By this point in the sale process, I had mentally accepted the fact I was going to leave El Paso. The tough parts were not knowing where I would end up, and leaving behind my management team, most of whom I had promoted into their jobs. I had assembled an outstanding team, and I knew I would miss them, as well as the hundreds of dedicated employees in the field who did a great job for the organization. I knew it was important to remain positive throughout this process, and I began to look forward to going with ANR Pipeline, still unsure of what lay ahead for me.

As I made presentations to each of the bidders about ANR's operations organization, I couldn't help but wonder who the successful bidder was going to be and whether or not I would be wanted as part of the organization. I saw three possible options for me.

First, the acquiring company might want me to continue with it, and possibly even in a larger role—particularly if the acquirer wasn't another natural gas transmission company. Several of the bidders were non-natural gas companies and would most likely need our experienced officer team to run the business. My current role could be expanded beyond just operations to include several other functions, such as engineering and technical services, which would be exciting and challenging.

Second, I could always take a job with another company. I wasn't sure I really wanted to start over with a new company, most likely in a different industry. My wife and I loved living in Nashville and didn't want to relocate at this time of our lives unless we had no other options.

Third, I could start my own company. I realized that this was the only option I had any real control over. Over the years, I had thought from time to time about starting my own company. But I also found it very difficult to walk away from a great job that paid well and offered other benefits that I wouldn't have if I worked for myself. I had always heard about "golden handcuffs" and how hard it was to leave a corporate job after getting to the officer level. I was 52 years old and knew that if I chose to start my own business, I probably needed to do so within the next year or two.

At this point in the process, I was hoping for the first scenario, and in a few more weeks I would find out whether it was to be.

We finished making presentations to all the bidders in early December. I was anxious to hear who the successful bidder was and, for selfish reasons, found myself hoping it would not be one of the pipeline companies. The news came on the morning of December 13: the successful bidder was

TransCanada Corporation, a large, natural gas transmission company based in Calgary—not the news I was hoping to hear. But I knew that TransCanada was a well-run organization that had been expanding its operations into the United States by acquisitions over the past few years. Later that day, I got a telephone call requesting that I come to Houston the next day to meet with Russ Girling, head of TransCanada's pipeline systems. He wanted to interview the five El Paso officers going with ANR Pipeline.

I flew to Houston the next morning and met offsite with Russ for the interview, because the announcement hadn't been made public. Everyone was still trying to keep the deal under wraps. I told him I was very interested in joining TransCanada. I also assured him that they had acquired a great asset and pipeline system in ANR, the strongest asset being the ANR employees. During our short discussion, he explained TransCanada, discussed how ANR would fit comfortably into its long-term strategy, and asked me several questions about what I wanted to do. The interview lasted thirty minutes, and he closed by saying that decisions about who would be part of the senior management team would be made during the following week. I was glad to hear that I would know my fate soon. The past few months had been difficult for me and my family. We were all anxious to get some closure. Now I would only have to wait a few more days and see what would happen to me and my career.

Although the interview had gone well from my perspective, I had spent the earlier part of my career in human resources interviewing hundreds of people, and something didn't feel right about the interview with Russ. The shortness of the interview made me suspect that it was largely an obligatory gesture and that they had already made up their minds about whom to select for officer positions. Over the next few days, my wife and I continued to pray about our situation while we waited to hear about the status of my job. I kept busy with work and getting ready for the rapidly approaching Christmas holiday.

On December 21, around 7PM, my cell phone rang. I could see by the caller's ID it was Jim Yardley, president of the El Paso Pipeline Group. My boss Dan reported to Jim, so I was surprised that Jim was calling me at home.

"David Jones," I answered.

"David, this is Jim Yardley—sorry to bother you at home."

"No problem, Jim, how are you doing?"

"Fine," he said, "And yourself?"

"I'm doing great, Jim. I'm almost done shopping, and I'm

ready for Christmas."

"David, I wanted to let you know that I just got off the phone with Russ Girling at TransCanada." Russ was Jim's counterpart at TransCanada. Jim went on to say, "Russ told me that you will not be one of the officers they will be retaining after the deal closes. I wanted to give you a heads-up, because Russ will be calling you in the next day or two to tell you the news."

"Jim, thanks for letting me know. I'm disappointed with their decision, but not totally surprised." The call quickly ended, and, apparently, so had my twenty-nine years in the energy industry. Jim's call had caught me off guard, and I felt like someone had just knocked the wind out of me. He didn't have to make that tough call that night, but he felt an obligation to give the officer group a heads-up. Despite the bad news, I appreciated his giving me advance notice.

My wife, Tanya, wasn't home at the time. She and our daughter Kim were out finishing up some last-minute Christmas shopping. As I waited for them to come home, I was alone in my thoughts. *How do I tell my wife and family? Why didn't TransCanada decide to keep me? What will I do now the rest of my career? Did Dan know Jim was calling me? Surely he knew?* I was not only hurt to hear the bad news but confused about how it was all coming down. I sent an e-mail from my BlackBerry to let Dan know about the call I just got from Jim, suspecting that he already knew about it. I knew Dan always checked his BlackBerry. Sure enough, a short while later, my cell phone rang; it was Dan. I wasn't emotionally ready to talk to him or anyone else just then, and I let the call go to my voice mail. A few minutes later, I listened to his message. He told me that he had no idea Jim was calling me with the news. Dan was surprised and disappointed by TransCanada's decision. He asked me to call him back, and I did—but not until the next day, when I felt like talking. My thoughts quickly turned to the other four El Paso officers who were slated to go with the sale of ANR. I wondered if they had received a similar call from Jim. If so, I hoped they fared better with TransCanada than I had. I sent e-mail messages from my BlackBerry to the other four officers, letting them know about my call and wishing them better luck. I only heard back from one of them that evening, and his fate was the same as mine. I knew he was disappointed as well, and I wondered if he felt as rejected as I did.

About an hour later, my wife and daughter walked into the house. Tanya looked at me and said, "What's wrong?" Apparently, I didn't do a good job of hiding my disappointment and hurt. It was written all over my face.

"Jim Yardley just called me and told me TransCanada isn't going to offer me a job," I said.

"I'm sorry," she said as she hugged me. "It's their loss. We will do fine—and God has better things in store for you." Tears were beginning to well up in my eyes, and I tried to pretend that the bad news didn't bother me. But, after twenty-nine years of marriage, I knew I wasn't fooling her: she could sense my disappointment, pain and hurt. As a Christian, I trusted God was going to take care of us as He always had. His fingerprints were all over my career, and I knew He wasn't going to stop guiding our lives now. One of my favorite verses, Proverbs 16:3, came to mind: "Commit your actions to the Lord, and your plans will succeed." As always, I greatly appreciated her encouragement and faith in me, but it was a sad and difficult evening for me, and one that I will never forget. It had certainly put a damper on our Christmas spirit.

The next morning, I was feeling better, and I started thinking about my future. I called Dan, who was very encouraging and supportive. He told me he wasn't aware that Jim was going to call me the evening before. Tanya and our two grown children remained encouraging and upbeat, reminding me that I had always wanted to start my own business—now I could. I knew they were right. We spent the afternoon Christmas shopping and had just gotten into our car in the mall parking lot when my cell phone rang. I didn't recognize the number, but I expected it was the call Jim told me I would be getting. It was.

Russ Girling and I exchanged a few pleasantries. He was cordial but quickly got to the purpose of the call. He told me they had decided to put another person over operations who was more familiar with TransCanada's processes and company culture. Then he surprised me by telling me they were considering me for some other positions within the company—possibly in Canada—and asked if I would be interested. I told him that I was certainly willing to keep all my options open but that my decision would depend upon the job and location, among other factors. He also mentioned that if a position didn't work out they would be interested in having me work a few months past the acquisition close date to help them with organizational transition issues. I told him that I would certainly consider it; my primary concern now was looking out for the ANR field employees and doing what I could to help them make a smooth transition from El Paso to TransCanada. He said someone from TransCanada would be contacting me after the holidays to discuss the next steps with me in more detail. And then the call was over.

At this point, I still held out some hope that I might have a chance to go to work for the new organization. After all, I had intimate knowledge of the company they were acquiring, having been the operations officer over it and two other large pipeline companies for the last five years. Before being promoted to vice president of operations five years earlier, I had spent three years commuting from Nashville, Tennessee, to Houston, Texas, each week to lead one of the merger transition teams during three major multi-billion-dollar mergers. These three mergers had made El Paso the largest natural gas transmission pipeline company in the United States and a major player in the energy business. Having held a key role in three previous mergers during which we had successfully made significant changes to the company's structure and processes, I was hoping TransCanada would recognize the value I could bring to it as they merged ANR into their organization.

As painful as it was to get that phone call a few days before Christmas, I was also relieved to know the out-come—no more waiting. My career with El Paso was about to end, and I didn't know what the future held for me if TransCanada didn't offer me another position in their organization—or even if they did. In the end, another job offer with TransCanada never materialized. I worked for

them for three months past the February 2007 close, helping with the transition. While working for TransCanada I
continued to use my El Paso office. It was awkward being
around my former El Paso employees for those three
months, more so for them than me, it seems. Not only
was I no longer their boss, but we didn't even work for the
same company anymore. I don't think they knew what to
say to me or how long I was going to be doing transition
work. When my last day, Friday, May 22, finally arrived, I
was relieved. I returned to the office the next morning and
loaded the boxes containing my personal belongings into
my car. I left my company keys, credit cards, and ID badge
on the division director's desk and walked out the office
door for the last time. As I heard the thud of the door closing behind me, I wondered what new doors lay ahead for
me. TransCanada treated me well during that time, but I
was glad when it was over. I was ready to move on. After
May 22, my last day with TransCanada, I was going to be
unemployed for the first time since graduating from college: not the most comforting thought for someone who
had just turned fifty-two and hadn't prepared a résumé or
sat for a job interview since college. But at least I was no longer on the corporate mental and emotional roller coaster I
had ridden for those tough, few, final months. I knew I had

had a great career with El Paso that had exceeded my own expectations and goals, and the company had treated me very fairly throughout the sale process.

But it was time to move on, to look forward to doing something different with my career and with my life. I was now free to pursue my dreams—to do anything I wanted to do. It was both exciting and a little unnerving at the same time. The last few months had been difficult not only for me but for my family as well. We had all been on the emotional roller coaster ride; surely it would end now. But I was wrong; the roller coaster ride was far from over.

I couldn't help but wonder why I had lost my job. I thought, I'm sure, like everyone: *It wouldn't happen to me.* Now it had. El Paso had been through a lot of organizational changes in the last ten years, and I had been in the middle of most of them. I knew corporate America had been undergoing a transformation that started during the 1980s' merger mania. The natural gas industry certainly wasn't immune; many mergers and consolidations had taken place in the last fifteen years, costing thousands of employees their jobs, and more would probably come in the years ahead.

CHAPTER TWO

A Changing World?

He who rejects change is the architect of decay.
The only human institution which rejects progress is the cemetery.

HAROLD WILSON

W hether you are terminated, down-sized, laid off, or right-sized, the cold hard fact is that you've been fired; and I've yet to meet anyone who wanted to get fired. I suppose that if you hate your job, your boss, and your coworkers, getting fired could be the best thing that could happen to you. Otherwise, getting fired is no fun. It's a traumatic, gut-wrenching, embarrass-ing event that affects not only the person getting fired, but the person's family and friends—even the coworkers who remain with the company. I'm not the first person to get fired and I won't be the last. More and more employees are losing their jobs every day in America. Whether we liked losing our jobs really doesn't matter, because it doesn't change the fact that we have. The more quickly we accept reality, the more quickly we can move on to bigger and better things. It's easy to feel as if you've been wronged or mistreated, but thinking and acting like a victim won't help. The business world has radically changed, and it will keep changing. Futurists are predicting that the job world that my children will work in will be radically different from what I've experienced for the last thirty years. I've had one career with one industry and one employer, but members of Generations X and Y are predicted to have eight to ten different *careers*—not jobs—in their lifetimes.

But I do think it helps to understand what has changed fundamentally in corporate America, as well as what's driving those changes. You can hardly read a newspaper today without seeing a story about another company that is being acquired or downsized, bringing with it employee terminations. It's happening all across America. While writing this chapter, my local newspaper had the following headlines:

"Pulaski Auto Supplier to Close, Layoff 105 Employees"

"Avon to Cut 2,400 Jobs in Restructuring"

"Shop at Home to Close, 200 Employees Lose their Jobs"

Headlines such as these can be seen in newspapers all across the country. Unfortunately, it's not something new. It's been happening for years, but some parts of the country have been hit much harder than others.

So why are so many employees losing their jobs?

Remembering the "Good Ole Days"

The business climate that organizations operate in today is significantly different from that of just twenty years ago—certainly from fifty years ago. Prior to the 1980s, American companies were relatively stable except during anomalous periods such as the Great Depression and the world wars. Most business growth was organic instead of through the mergers and acquisitions that are commonplace today. Most businesses back then didn't change drastically. Wall Street's expectations were lower, and global competition wasn't the factor it is today. Countries like Japan and China were just beginning to produce products that could compete with American goods. In fact, most products from these countries were considered cheap junk, certainly inferior to American-made products. The technological revolution was just beginning. Computers were in their infancy and used only by the few large companies that could afford them. Automation and robotics were fairly rare and were limited primarily to high-tech firms.

When an employee hired on with an organization, it wasn't unusual to expect to remain there until retirement: from cradle to grave. Employees expected loyalty from their employers in return for their loyalty. I know many retirees who spent their entire careers, many more than forty years, working for one company. Companies promulgated this mindset and developed many of their employee benefit plans with long-term employment in mind. Defined pension plans promised employees annuity payments after retirement based on factors such as years of service, final average pay, and age at retirement. The formula was simple: the more years you worked, the more you were paid upon retirement. Larger companies routinely offered retiree medical benefits at little or no cost to retirees—a rarity these days. Frankly, those were the "good ole days." Times have certainly changed, and so have organizations. The "good ole days" are now the "gone ole days."

Welcome to the Real World

Today, companies are under intense pressures from Wall Street, shareholders, regulators, and competitors. Wall Street expects earnings to improve each quarter. It likes to see companies cut costs—including labor costs—through mergers, downsizings, and other such things. But the Street doesn't care about the effect these cuts have on employees who lose their jobs, or about the internal chaos created during mergers and the declining morale of the employees who remain. Pressure from the investment community often forces businesses to make poor short-term decisions at the expense of sound long-term strategies. This philosphy unfortunately can lead to bankruptcy and thousands of employees not only losing their jobs, but their pensions and savings.

Shareholders also have higher expectations from companies today. Investing in companies because they pay a good dividend each quarter is no longer in vogue with most investors. Many investors only want to see the share price increase yearly and shy away from stocks that pay a dividend in favor of growth stocks.

The implied expectation from the Street each quarter is "perform or perish." An article in *Fortune* magazine pointed out that on the July 1955 list of Fortune 500 companies, only seventy-one are still on the list today. Thirteen of the top twenty companies then are no longer on the list now, for one reason or another. Today, the average lifespan of a company in the United States is approximately forty years. In Japan and Europe, it is only 12½. That means that when someone hires on with a U.S. company that has been around for thirty years, on average the employee can only expect to work there for ten more years—not for the rest of his or her career.

Companies are facing tougher regulations, particularly environmental and financial ones. It's not uncommon today for it to take longer for a company to obtain all of its required environmental permits than to complete the construction of a major project. Regulatory compliance costs American companies billions of dollars each year (Colvin 2004).

Competition is also much tougher today. Companies are no longer able to compete only domestically. Nowadays, they must compete globally, in large part because of technology that lowers transportation costs and shortens production cycles and new product development times. Consequently, many U.S. manufacturing industries are struggling to compete with products manufactured by inexpensive labor in countries such as Mexico, Vietnam, Thailand, and China.

Technology Enables Change

We now live in the information age, and it has changed our world forever. We play, work, and communicate differently. E-mails, text messaging, blogs, and twitters are the new tools of communication. Computers and the Internet have made our world smaller by changing the way companies do business and interact with their customers. Technology is all around us: we can't escape it. It dominates our lives and has simplified many of the things we do, but it has simultaneously complicated our lives, exposing us to overwhelming amounts of information each day, whether at work or at home. Information overload is here to stay.

It wasn't that long ago that leaving work at the end of the day meant forgetting about it until the next morning. Today, that's practically impossible. Cell phones, pagers, BlackBerrys, and other devices keep us constantly connected to our jobs. I can't count the number of times I've responded to a text message while sitting at dinner, in a meeting, or, occasionally, in a vehicle, driving down the road (I don't recommend the last). E-mails and text messages are controlling our lives and marginalizing our free time. It's not unusual for employees to send and receive one hundred e-mails or more each day. It's almost impossible not to take your PC with you on vacation today to keep up with the constant stream of e-mails back at the office. Otherwise, when you return from a weeklong vacation, it takes days to read all your e-mails and to simply catch up. Vacations that allow you to completely get away from work are a thing of the past—at least for professional employees.

Technology and automation have changed how many jobs need to be done today. Vehicles, by way of example, are manufactured largely by robots and sophisticated computerized machines that stamp out parts, make welds, and perform other tasks that employees used to do. ATM machines have replaced thousands of bank tellers. Full-service gas stations are hard to find. Remember when people used to answer a company's telephone, instead of a voice recording with a host of options to navigate through before transferring callers to an actual person if they have the patience to make it that far?

The combination of these changes has made it more and more difficult for companies to compete and to succeed. Companies are under constant pressure to increase revenues and reduce costs, constantly looking for ways to achieve economics of scale and maximize their competitive advantages. Many companies find that the easiest way to do this, and to do it quickly, is not via organic growth but rather through mergers and acquisitions. For the last two decades, we have seen the number of mergers grow exponentially. During the last ten years I worked for El Paso Corporation, we went through three major mergers in which thousands of employees lost their jobs. Mergers naturally create synergy but result in overlapped services, redundant jobs, and duplicated processes, giving companies little choice but to terminate excess employees in order to lower operating costs, reduce corporate debt, and increase operating efficiency.

When companies aren't merging, they are constantly looking for ways to be more competitive, which usually means reducing operating costs. When I started in 1977, the terms re-engineering, downsizing, right-sizing, outsourcing, and a host of others didn't even exist. Now they are commonplace. Collectively, all these business dynamics and changes have caused companies to think differently about how they view their employees. Many companies no longer see employees as assets but as expenses necessary for doing business. Employee salaries are certainly a large expense item on the balance sheet, as are other employee-related expenses, such as benefits. Employee benefit costs have skyrocketed over the last decade—especially health care. Most companies have been forced to make major changes to their benefit packages by replacing costly long-term plans such as defined pensions with cash balance plans, eliminating or reducing retiree medical plans, pushing cost-sharing of health care premiums with employees, reducing 401(k) matches, and completely eliminating other employee benefits.

Just as employers have changed their way of viewing their employees, employees, too, have changed their views of their employers. Mergers, layoffs, downsizings, and other restructuring efforts over the last two decades have cost millions of employees their jobs. As a consequence, employees often no longer feel a sense of loyalty to their employers. Sure, most employees still appreciate the companies they work for and are thankful for the benefits they do have. They realize, however, their employment is more tenuous than ever and that, at any moment, they could find themselves unemployed. They have watched too many family members, friends, coworkers, and neighbors lose their jobs. It's easy to understand why they no longer trust their employers as they once did.

Rob's Story

The following testimony describes an all too common scenario in the workforce today.

I worked for a large health care company. They had recently gone through a leveraged buyout and were struggling financially. It seems that all the departments had been given the mandate to cut their budgets by 20 percent to reduce operating costs. One Monday morning, they terminated a lot of employees in each department. I happened to be out of town that day, but I quickly heard the news. When I returned to the office the following day, I got a call from my department VP, who said she wanted to meet with me. She told me she had just bought a book as a gift for her husband and wanted to show it to me to see if I thought he would like it. I went to her office and she showed me the book, which was a devotional book. As I was looking at the book and making some comments about it, she slid a large envelope across her desk and in front of me. She told me it was my severance package. I was shocked and didn't know what to say. I had been around the corporate world long enough to know that if the decision had been made, nothing I could say or do would change their minds. I got up and took the package back to my office, still not able to believe this was happening to me. I started to cry and wondered what I was going to do. The reason I had missed the cuts the day before was that my wife and I had just moved my father from Oklahoma to be closer to us. He was struggling with some serious personal addiction problems and the effects of a recent stroke, and we wanted to be closer to him so we could take better care of him. Now, not only were we dealing with the added responsibility of caring for my dad, but I had to also deal with the pressure of losing my job.

The company asked me to leave the premises that day, but before I left they told me to take my company PC with me. I provided IT support for my department, and they wanted me to continue to provide some reports I had developed that year for my department. I thought, *You just fired me, but you still want to me do some work for you!* After leaving the company, I was never really angry at them for letting me go. I really didn't have time to be angry or depressed, because I made up my mind that I was going to find another job quickly. Finding a job became my new job, and I worked hard to find something else. I knew networking was important, so I started networking like crazy and just kept calling people back to follow up on leads. I was so persistent that one person I kept calling told me to come and visit him so that we could talk—*if* I promised to stop calling him. We had a great conversation, and he really helped me to think about what I wanted to do—and I did stop calling him.

I found another job in about two months by networking. It was a difficult time, and I learned a lot about myself and others. I was surprised by how some of my peers at my old company treated me after I left. One of them lives near me, and I ran into him one day—he wouldn't even speak to me but looked the other way and pretended not to see me. I've tried several times to call my old boss, who has yet to return my phone calls. Looking back, the good thing about being unemployed for a couple of months was the opportunity it afforded to spend some quality time with my dad, who died a few months ago, which means that I lost my job, my dad, my mother, and my grandmother all within the past couple years. It's been hard, but life goes on. However, I am now in a job that I love and feel passionate about. It wasn't the job I took after being terminated, but I kept looking for the opportunity to move into my current position. I'm glad I didn't settle for just any job. I targeted this job and actively pursued it.

CHAPTER THREE

A Roller Coaster Ride

Give your stress wings, and let it fly away.

CARIN HARTNESS

S ince being fired, I've talked to many other people who have also lost their jobs. Few of them saw it coming. You never think you're going to be fired, so you're usually not prepared for it when it happens. Even though I knew when I was going through the disposition of ANR Pipeline that there was a possibility I could lose my job, I really didn't think it would happen. When it did happen, I was surprised; even though I thought I was prepared mentally and emotionally, I quickly found out that I wasn't. But I was more prepared than people are who have no clue that they're going to be terminated until it actually happens.

I wasn't prepared, however, for the wave of emotions I rode for the couple of months that followed my termination. It was like riding an emotional roller coaster. My experience wasn't unique. Others have shared their experiences with me, and theirs weren't much different than mine. When you're riding the emotional roller coaster, one minute you're headed up, and everything looks bright and sunny; the next minute, you're spiraling downward, feeling out of control. Eventually the roller coaster comes to a stop, and you climb off and move on to the next thing in your life. A friend of mine likened it to being stranded in a small boat at sea during a storm. He said you feel you have virtually no control over the boat. You're being tossed about by the sea at will—rising one moment on a surging wave and then quickly plummeting as the wave passes. You know the storm will eventually end, but you don't know when. About the time you think the storm is over, another squall line comes through, and the sea gets rough again. Eventually the waves die down, and the storm passes, revealing blue skies once again.

The emotional roller coaster you go through after being terminated is normal. Everyone who loses a job experiences it. You're neither alone nor unique. After all, being fired is a stressful event. One article I read recently listed the ten most stressful things a person goes through during the course of an ordinary life:

Top 10 Life Stressors

1. Death of a spouse
2. Divorce
3. Marital separation
4. Jail term or death of a close family member
5. Personal injury or illness
6. Marriage
7. **Loss of a job due to termination**
8. Marital reconciliation or retirement
9. Pregnancy
10. Change in financial state

Loss of a job due to termination ranks seventh on the list. Obviously, after losing your job, you will be under some financial pressure—and change in financial state ranks number ten (Frey 2008). It's fine to be stressed about what you're going through. It's normal, and it is to be expected. Accepting that fact helps you cope. Congratulations, you get to experience two of life's top ten stressors simultaneously.

When I was fired, my last day with TransCanada was May 22. My father-in-law had died of a heart attack just four weeks earlier. We were also in the process of building a new home at the time of my termination while trying to sell our house in a bleak real estate market. Later that same year, our daughter got married (paying for a wedding can cause number ten on the list), and our son got engaged. My wife and I figured that after surviving all of those things in one year by the grace of God, life could only get better. It has.

Losing your job is stressful, and it can be life-changing. For most people, it's a period of grief. Many people think grieving is limited only to losing a loved one or to being terminally ill. That's simply not true. Any traumatic event in a person's life can cause grief and bring a wide range of feelings, from shock to depression. This cycle of feeling is often referred to as the grief cycle, an idea originally developed to help people understand the emotions they experience after the death of a loved one. The emotions you experience after losing a job are very similar and often follow the same stages in the grief cycle. You will experience some of—and possibly all—of the stages. Nearly everyone who loses their job does, but to varying degrees—and not necessarily in the same order. The length and order of each stage varies with each person.

Fortunately, several years ago I was trained by my pastor about the grief cycle. I'm a deacon in my church, and we occasionally minister to families in our congregation who go through tragedies such as divorce or the loss of a spouse. Knowing about the cycle helped me as I went through some of its stages during my job loss. The model that follows was developed by Dr. Elisabeth Kubler-Ross, a famous psychiatrist and author from Switzerland whose 1969 book *On Death and Dying* helped change people's view of tragedy and grief. She designed the model to help describe the stages in any catastrophic event in a person's life, such as job loss, divorce, illness, or the death of a loved one.

As the grief cycle shows, losing your job can put you on an emotional roller coaster as you struggle to cope with the change. The cycle has five stages that range from denial to acceptance. It is helpful to understand each stage, as well as the emotions you will encounter as you go through the cycle.

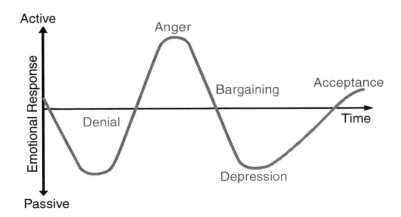

Stages of the Grief Cycle

1. Denial: This is the initial stage. When we are in denial, we don't want to believe what is happening to us. We may be in shock and can't believe we just lost our job. This is particularly true when we didn't see it coming and felt secure in our jobs, going to work on the fateful day expecting it to be like any other day until the boss walks into your office, or calls you into his, to drop the bomb: you're terminated. You can't believe this is really happening. You feel totally numb, as if someone just hit you with an emotional Taser. You hear the words coming out of your manager's mouth, but you can't really believe them. Your work day (and life) just went from normal to nightmarish. Thoughts begin to rush through your mind: "this can't be happening"; "I'm dreaming this"; "why me?"; "what will I tell my wife and kids?"; "my career is over."

You probably liked having a structured work routine. Most of us like structure in our lives and find comfort in certain routines. Little things, like reading the newspaper in the morning, taking the same route to our workplace each day, or having our first cup of coffee after getting to work, provide us with a comfort zone. Now the structured routine we became accustomed to no longer exists. We have no job to go to, no coworkers to chat with, no normal job duties. We still read the newspaper, but now it's the employment ads.

You may find it easier to deny what's happening to you than to accept it. There can be different types of denial, including denial of fact, denial of responsibility, and denial of denial. One of the most common reactions during the denial stage is embarrassment.

Even though I knew losing my job was totally out of my control and had nothing to do with my performance or abilities, I was still embarrassed that it had happened to me. I felt like I had let my family down in some strange way. It was embarrassing to tell my wife, my children, and my father that I had lost my job even though they knew, as I did, that my job was at risk, and that it wasn't my fault.

It was also embarrassing to tell my friends I had lost my job even though I knew they weren't going to stop being my friends just because I was unemployed. I wasn't sure what to tell anyone. I didn't like the words "fired" or "terminated"; "lost my job" sounded less embarrassing to me. Mentally, it seemed as though I was walking around with a flashing neon sign on my chest that read "I'm unemployed." For the first few weeks, whenever I was in a social setting, I hoped no one asked me where I worked or what I did for a living. Of course, when they did, I stumbled to find an answer.

How to deal with shock and denial

As a friend of mine told me, after losing her job, she just wanted to crawl into a hole and sleep, hoping that when she awoke, everything would be back to normal again. Shock and denial are normal and natural reactions when you lose your job. You will need time to recover and recuperate from the bad news. Make sure you do this—and that you do it in your own way. It gives you a chance to catch your emotional and mental breath, which will allow you to respond rather than to react to your situation. There is a difference between responding and reacting: response is positive, but reaction is negative. Someone being treated for a serious disease likes to hear the doctor say, "Your body is responding to your treatments" rather than "Your body is reacting to your treatments." People who react to being fired often do so in an uncontrolled manner. They blow their tops and may verbally or even physically lash out at people—including those they love.

It's not unusual during this stage to start worrying, letting fear set in. You may find yourself worrying about finding another job, paying your bills, having to possibly move to another city, or about a host of other things. Worrying about what you're going to do now and how you're going to maintain your livelihood is a perfectly acceptable response.

Worry can easily turn into fear, however, and if we aren't careful, fear can paralyze our ability to think and act rationally. The good news is that most of the things we worry about never happen. Someone once told me that worry is nothing more than negative goal setting. He was right.

2. Anger: During the second stage, we begin to feel that we shouldn't have lost our jobs or that what happened to us wasn't fair. We feel as if we are victims, and we can easily take on the victim mentality. We want to hold someone else responsible for what happened, whether it be our boss, the company in general, or even other people or circumstances. During this stage, our anger may be directed toward God, the person who fired us, friends, family members, peers, coworkers, or even ourselves. It's normal to be angry about how we were treated (or not treated) by the company. We may feel that the company didn't give us enough severance, that it failed to show any compassion, or that it didn't treat us humanely enough.

After I was fired, I was angry for a few days. My anger was never targeted at my boss, who was supportive and caring through the entire process and who remains a friend today. I wasn't angry at El Paso for not retaining me after TransCanada didn't offer me a job. My anger was directed more at TransCanada; I believed they didn't give me enough consideration for a possible job with their company and that they didn't value what I could bring to their organization. Now, I can look back at their decision and realize that, had I been in their shoes, I would probably have also picked a person familiar with their own organization to lead operations. They also knew that I didn't want to relocate from the Nashville area, which wasn't an ideal situation for them.

As a business leader, I've been on the other side of the firing situation numerous times in my career. I know from experience that firing someone, even for just cause, is a very difficult and stressful situation for a boss, too. I found it to be the most difficult thing I ever did as a manager. I always tried to be as professional and compassionate as I could, but despite my best efforts I always felt I fell short. Human resource professionals train managers to be as humane as possible while making the termination conversation a short one. Dragging out the termination conversation is painful and nonproductive for both the manager and the employee being terminated. Some people, when told they are terminated, want to debate on the spot the reason they're being fired. However, arguing with the boss or making a big scene doesn't help and will not change the outcome. You can argue until you're blue in the face, but guess what—you're still fired. It's much better (though not necessarily easier) to take the high road when being fired than to burn your bridges.

By stage two, we've had enough time to move past denial and shock; the numbness has worn off, and we begin mentally to rationalize what has happened to us. Often the thoughts of fear and anxiety that began in stage one continue during this stage and can become even worse. We may begin to question our own abilities and may even find it difficult to make routine decisions.

As Kubler-Ross states, "Anger surfaces once you are feeling safe enough to know you will probably survive whatever comes." Anger is a normal and necessary part of grieving; once you get through it, you will start to heal. It's important not to let anger turn into bitterness. Bitterness is like a cancer that eats away inside you, hurting the one harboring the bitterness the most. Don't become bitter—I guarantee you it will not help you *or* your situation.

How to deal with anger

People express and deal with anger in various ways. Some people blow up and get mad at everything and everyone; others cry or even weep; some internalize it and show little external emotion. People who internalize their feelings must be careful, for internalization can lead to physical problems such as ulcers, anxiety attacks, and hypertension—to name a few. It's important to deal with your anger; but do it in a way that doesn't impact others. If shouting is how you usually cope with anger, go somewhere where you can be alone, and shout it out. Get it off your chest. If you need to, buy a punching bag and hit it until your fists hurt, or beat on a pillow or cushion. It helps to vent your anger. The quicker you can move past the anger stage, the better it is for you and for those around you. Just make sure that if you're angry, you control and channel your anger in a positive and constructive fashion. Sadly, we have seen too many instances in our country where a terminated employee "goes postal," sometimes even resorting to deadly violence after being fired.

You may find it helpful to talk to someone you can openly and candidly share your feelings with. The person can be a family member, friend, pastor, or counselor. The support and encouragement of that person, and of others, can be a great help to you. Some people find it helpful to keep a journal or to make a list of the things they are upset with or worrying about. If you do this, share your list with the person you are talking to. They can help you put things in perspective and identify which of your worries are valid and which ones aren't. This is also the best time to address the inevitable "what if" scenarios entering your mind: What if I can't find a new job? What if my spouse and I can't pay our bills? What if we have to move to another city? What if we have to sell our house? By thinking through or discussing the what-ifs, you will have already thought through situations if they happen, and may have developed an action plan to effectively address them.

3. **Bargaining:** Once you've moved beyond the anger stage, you feel better now, having gotten much of the negative thoughts and feelings off of your chest and out of your mind. In the bargaining stage, you start to play mental games with yourself. You can easily fool yourself into thinking that unrealistic things may happen: "Maybe the company will realize they made a mistake and will call me back and offer me another job"; "I will find a new job quickly." You find yourself mentally replaying things you did in your past job that you will do differently or better in your next job. You begin to think about job possibilities that you feel confident will work out for you, or you convince yourself that if you talk to a certain high level business friend or acquaintance, they will offer you a job. After all, they know you well and know of your abilities; why wouldn't they want to hire you? Plus, they know you need a job—surely they will want to help you. During the bargaining stage,

you start to look for the knight on the white horse who will ride up to you at any moment and rescue you by offering you a great job that solves all your immediate problems. Mentally bargaining usually leads to false hopes and unfulfilled expectations.

How to deal with bargaining

This can be a difficult stage for many people. They begin to have some hope that things will work out, because they believe that something or someone is going to come along and fix things for them. I'm not saying that it can't happen, but it seldom does. Hope is a good thing, but it's a poor strategy for finding another job. It's at this point in the cycle that you have to realize that it's up to you to find yourself another job. It's your responsibility, not anyone else's. *You* have to make it happen. You need to remain positive and realize it may take some time—possibly several months—to find another job. Often there is a correlation between age and salary and the time it takes to find another job. The cold, hard fact is that the older you are, the higher your salary, and the more you restrict yourself geographically or by industry, the longer it is going to take you to find a comparable job.

This can be a frustrating stage. It was for me when I lost

my job. You may find that a lot of friends and coworkers quickly forget about you. Many of the people you worked with for years will not even bother to call you or to drop you a quick note or e-mail to simply say hello and see how you're doing. Even more painful, some of them may not even return your phone calls or e-mails. A friend of mine who was president of a company and lost his job reports, "People will not return my phone calls or respond to my e-mails. Many of these people were people that I helped out at one time or another when they needed it." Most of your coworkers, unless you see them socially or bump into them at stores, movie theaters, or elsewhere, will never contact you again. It's almost like you died or have some socially contagious disease. If you contact them or bump into them, expect to hear things like, "I was thinking about you the other day" or "I've been meaning to give you a call"—and hope that they were, though for some reason they never found the time.

You can't help but think that your company, coworkers, and subordinates will miss you. They may for a short period of time, but rest assured that both you and your contribution will be quickly forgotten. Someone once told me a great analogy regarding this. She said, "Imagine sticking your hand in a bucket of water; then pull out your hand. The hole left when you remove your hand is how much you will be missed after you're gone." I have news for you—no one is irreplace-able in the business world. Why do your coworkers fail to contact you or to stay in touch? I think this happens because the people you worked with often feel they don't know the right words to say to you after you've left, or they get caught up in fighting their own fires each day and don't make the time to contact you. They may want to, but the next thing they know, it's been months since you left, and they are too embarrassed to get in touch by then. The old saying is sad but true: out of sight, out of mind.

I was hurt by some friends who I felt abandoned me after I left my job. However, I look back on my own career and recall friends I worked with who lost their jobs before me. I valued their friendships and hated to see them leave, but I never took the time to follow-up on them to see how they were doing or what I could do to help them. I had planned to, but never got around to doing it—a simple act of car-ing. I deeply regret it now. I am much more sensitive now to other people who lose their jobs or who are struggling in general. Making time for them is now a priority with me—but I learned that lesson the hard way.

4. Depression: When we begin to dwell on what has happened to us and choose to become martyrs, or when we struggle to find another job, we can easily fall into the pit of depression. As depression sets in, we often become sad or despondent and may feel as if nothing else matters in our lives. We blame ourselves for being terminated and mentally replay constantly all the bad things from our past. The rear-view mirror of life becomes our focus, making forward movement extremely difficult. We begin to see ourselves as unworthy and as deserving of our plight. It becomes one pity party after another as we picture ourselves as losers in life. The sad thing is that lapsing into depression not only hurts us but those around us, particularly our families. If we're not careful, it can create marital problems and even lead to separation, divorce, or thoughts of suicide, which can cause us to become even more depressed.

Symptoms of depression can include:

- Intense feelings of guilt
- Suicidal thoughts
- Slow movements and speech
- Difficulty sleeping
- Sleeping too much
- Inability to start looking for a new job
- Trouble functioning at social events
- Inability to complete normal, daily tasks
- Loss of appetite

How to deal with depression

Fortunately, not everyone who loses a job goes through depression, and most who do come out of it quickly. This stage can often be avoided by having a good support group in place consisting of your family, friends, church, and an outplacement service. It's easier to avoid this stage or break out of it with the help of others than it is to try to do it alone. There are several things you can do to help escape the grip depression can have on you.

First, stop blaming yourself for what happened. As much as we would like to be in control of everything, many things in our lives are beyond our control. You're not alone in what you're experiencing. Thousands of people are losing their jobs just like you and me because they simply happened to be in the wrong place at the wrong time. In my case, I couldn't help it if my company decided to sell one of the companies I was responsible for running. It also wasn't my fault that the new buyer decided to select someone else to run Operations.

Second, if you're a person of faith, put your faith to work. Being a Christian helped me cope. I knew God was in control of my life and that He had bigger and better things in store for me. The time I spent reading the Bible and praying was a huge help. As I studied the scriptures, these great verses of promise were comforting and reassuring to me:

"Cast all your cares upon God, because He cares about you."

I Peter 5:7

"Trust in the Lord with all your heart, and do not rely on your own understanding; think about Him in all your ways, and He will guide you on the right paths."

Proverbs 3:5

"Commit your activities to the Lord and your plans will be achieved."

Proverbs 16:3

Third, stop focusing totally on yourself and focus on others. Do something to help someone else. Shifting the focus of your thoughts and actions to other people will get you out of the rut you're in. You can't help but feel better about yourself when you help someone else who is in need. Your local church, as well as numerous charities and volunteer organizations, would welcome your help.

Fourth, get moving. Stop sitting around, drowning in a pool of pity. Get up and take a walk. Notice the sights and sounds of nature. Exercise is great therapy and a wonderful stress reliever. You will be surprised at how much better you feel after a good walk or jog. Remember: motion helps create energy. As professional golfer Gary Player likes to say, "Rest too much, and you start to rust."

Fifth, if you're experiencing severe depression, I strongly encourage you to <u>get professional help and treatment</u>.

5. **Acceptance:** The quicker we get to this stage, the better. Acceptance certainly doesn't mean that we like or agree with what has happened to us, but it does mean that we're ready to move on with our lives and our careers. Getting to this point doesn't mean that a job will show up in the mail the next day to solve all our problems. We're still facing the daily reality of being unemployed, but now we're taking proactive steps to deal with our situation. Keep in mind that being in this stage doesn't mean that we can't slip back into previous stages of the grief cycle. I've talked to several people who thought they had a job in the bag, only to see it fail to come to fruition. As a result, they were extremely disappointed and found themselves going through some of the earlier stages of the grief cycle once again. You're climbing a slippery slope, but keep climbing—even if you slide backward for a short time. You'll get to the top in the end.

How to deal with acceptance

Being in the final stage of the cycle doesn't mean we've made it. We are still unemployed and dealing with the issues that naturally brings. However, short of being employed, it's where we want to be because we've made it to the end of the grief cycle. But even though we accept what has happened and

> *We are free up to the point of choice, then the choice controls the chooser.*
>
> MARY CROWLEY

see some light at the end of our tunnel, it doesn't mean that our career detour is over or that there won't be some more bumps in the road ahead. There will still be mood swings, ups-and-downs, good days, bad days. These continue for most people until they find a new job.

There is Light at the End of the Tunnel

Losing a job is a traumatic event that affects each person differently. It's the world we live in. We can't change it or control it, but we do control something very powerful: we control the choices we make when something happens to us. Are we going to respond or react to our situation? There is a huge difference between the two responses.

I'm reminded of a story told by Zig Ziglar, the great motivational speaker from Dallas, Texas. Zig had just finished a seminar and was at the airport catching his return flight home. When he got to the ticket counter to check his bags, the ticket agent announced that his flight to Dallas was going to be delayed until 7:30PM, a four-hour delay, even though the plane was parked at the gate. Ziglar immediately responded in typical Zig fashion. "That's fantastic!" he said, with a smile on his face. The ticket agent was shocked at his positive response and said, "Sir, did you just say that was 'fantastic'?" "Yes, ma'am, I did," Zig responded. "It's fantastic!" The ticket agent said, "Sir, that's what I thought you said. But why in the world would you respond in such a way when I just gave you bad news? After all, I'm sure you're not excited about getting to Dallas late." Zig replied, "I do want to get home, but since the plane is delayed, I figure one of three things must be happening. One, there is something wrong with the plane. Two, there is something wrong up there in the sky where that plane is going to fly. Or three, there is something wrong with one of the pilots who is going to fly that plane. The way I look at it is, if any of those three things are true, I'd much rather be right here safe on the ground than on that plane. After all, this is a beautiful terminal and I have plenty of things I can do while I wait. I can get something to eat at that fine restaurant over there, then grab a comfortable chair and get some work done. Fantastic!" In telling this story, Zig says he could have chosen a different approach. He says, "I could have gotten upset with the ticket agent and given her a piece of my mind. I could have, but the plane still wouldn't have left until 7:30 PM; I could have raised my voice, pounded my fist on the counter, and made a big scene, but the plane still wouldn't have left until 7:30 PM; I could have demanded to have seen her manager or someone else in authority, but the plane still wouldn't have left until 7:30 PM; or I could have demanded that my scheduled flight leave on time like it was supposed to have done, but the plane still wouldn't have left until 7:30 PM." Zig says, "I could have done all those things, but no matter what I did or said didn't change the fact that my plane was still going to leave at 7:30 PM, not one minute earlier." Zig chose to respond to his situation—not to react to it.

You might be thinking, "David, you can't compare losing my job to Ziglar's plane being delayed." I agree—the situations are different. But, just like Zig, you and I have a choice to make. We can choose to react as a victim: to be angry and upset about losing our jobs. We can demand our jobs back. We can get mad, shout, stomp our feet, and cry foul at the top of our lungs. We can do all those things. The only problem with those choices is that they don't solve our problem or make it any better. Yes, we can do all those things, but WE HAVE STILL LOST OUR JOBS.

But we can make another choice. We can decide to respond like victors. A victor is someone who accepts reality (it doesn't mean liking it!) and consciously decides to make the best of it, no matter what. We can cope constructively with our feelings. We can develop a plan of action and find another job. We can move on and not look back.

Which response do you choose? I hope you make the decision to be a victor and move forward with your career and your life. I did, and so can you! But before we start developing our plan of action, I want to suggest to you some people who can and should be a part of your support team.

Tom's Story

I've worked in the health care industry my entire career. I've had a great career and enjoyed success in every job I've had. My family and I've moved around several times and were in North Carolina for sixteen years. I had a great job there with a leading hospital where I was over all the physician and clinical practices for the hospital, reporting to the CEO. My wife had a great job also, and my daughter was a freshman in high school. One year ago I was recruited by another large, nationally recognized hospital in Texas to join them as COO. It was a great opportunity, and the hospital and new CEO both had outstanding reputations in the industry. We decided it was a great career move for me, so we uprooted from a community we had grown to love to move to Texas.

The day after I started work, I found out we had serious problems with one of the more profitable practices within our hospital. Consequently, a number of well-known highly specialized doctors left the hospital, which had a huge financial impact on the hospital. The executive team had decided the hospital needed to cut about 150 employees, including several department heads. So my first week was spent terminating employees and dealing with major morale issues among other challenges. We spent most of the year going through restructuring and right-sizing efforts to stop the financial hemorrhaging. I remember that in May, my CEO publicly told hospital employees how great a job I was doing and how much he appreciated my leadership. The next week I happened to be on vacation and got an ugly e-mail from him that made no sense to me. I began to sense that something was wrong. Two months later, the CEO told me that he was combining my area with another area and eliminating my job. He told me that with my background and track record I would have no trouble finding another job in town. One month later, I was unemployed and still trying to figure out what had happened. Only a year ago, I had uprooted my family and sold our dream home to take what appeared to be a great job, only to find myself looking for a job for the first time in my career.

Within weeks of leaving, I had several job interviews, several of which looked extremely promising. One company all but offered me a job but needed to work through a few details. I was very encouraged and it looked as if things were going to work out after all. That was ten months ago, and they haven't worked out. Now I feel as if I've hit a wall, and it's easy to get discouraged. I haven't slept well since the day I was told I was being terminated. I have two kids in college and one in a private high school. I need to find another job soon. I've been networking and talking to everyone I can talk to, and now I'm looking for jobs in other states even though we don't want to move. We may not have any other option. I have been surprised at the way my peers at the hospital have treated me after leaving. Not a one of them has reached out to me, and many will not even return my phone calls. It's as if I have some contagious disease.

CHAPTER FOUR

Don't Fly Solo

We are pressed on every side by troubles, but we are not crushed.
We are perplexed, but not driven to despair.
We are hunted down, but never abandoned by God.
We get knocked down, but we are not destroyed.

2 CORINTHIANS 4:8–9

A few years ago, I decided to pursue another goal on my 107 List and get my pilot's license. Since college I had wanted to learn to fly a plane but kept putting it off for one reason or another. As my son grew older, it was clear he wanted to become a pilot, which he has now done. He is a pilot for one of the regional carriers. After getting his pilot's license, he talked me into taking flying lessons. It was fun and challenging, and I was achieving a lifelong goal. On my ninth lesson, my instructor told me to land the plane, which I did. To my surprise, he opened his door, stepped out of the plane and said, "You're ready to solo." Solo! I'm glad he thought I was ready, but at that moment I wasn't so sure. He assured me I could do it. After all, I had about ten hours of flight time under my belt and I had completed numerous takeoffs and landings. He was right about all those things, but he forgot to mention that he had been sitting in the seat next to me every hour I had flown. I knew if anything went wrong he was ready to bail me out, keeping us out of trouble. Now, it was up to me—and me alone. He closed the door, and I taxied out to the end of the runway and was cleared by the tower for takeoff. I went through all my pre-takeoff checks, and then I rolled onto the runway, revved the engine, and started down the runway. I'm not sure what was revving the fastest—the plane's engine or my heart! When I reached my takeoff speed, I pulled the yoke back, and the Cessna rose slowly into the air—so far, so good. During the flight in the traffic pattern, I was in contact via radio with my instructor who was in the tower watching me along with the air traffic controller. My son surprised me and was in the tower, too. A thunderstorm had been developing a few miles east of the airport, but it wasn't expected to head our way. As I got to the desired altitude, I noticed that the storm appeared to be headed toward the airport and that the winds were picking up. The controller instructed me to circle and land on the same runway from which I had just taken off. As I was turning on the downwind leg, he said that the winds had shifted and that I needed to land on a different runway. I had enough things racing through my mind (like *Why am I doing this?*) already without having to change my flight pattern and set up for a different runway. As I lined up for the new approach, I noticed that the plane was getting bumped around by the approaching storm. My instructor assured me that everything was fine but told me that I needed to land the plane

> "Any landing you walk away from is a good landing."

because of the storm. It had started to lightly rain, and if I missed the approach and had to go around for another landing, I would probably find myself in a thunderstorm. How's that for pressure? I made my final turn and lined the plane up with the runway. I had a fairly strong crosswind and it was starting to rain harder. I had been trained to land in crosswinds, but didn't like crosswind landings, not to mention that I wasn't great at them. But I did what I had been trained to do and turned the nose into the wind, correcting my heading by using the rudder. I quickly went through my landing checklist and kept heading the plane toward my landing spot while watching my approach speed to avoid stalling the plane. My heart was still racing, and I remember gripping the yoke as if I were trying to strangle it. I successfully landed the plane, and as I taxied to the hangar, it started to rain hard, with the wind gusting badly. I was grateful to be on the ground and in one piece. It hadn't been my best landing, but, as my son always told me, "any landing you walk away from is a good landing." When I climbed out of the plane my chest was hurting. No, I wasn't having a heart attack, but I had been so tense while landing the plane that I had gripped the yoke hard enough to pull a chest muscle. Despite the pulled muscle, I had successfully soloed.

Use Your Support Team

Losing your job can be a lot like soloing for the first time. You feel all alone and nervous because you're not sure how or where you're going to land. Although you may feel like you're flying solo after being terminated, the good news is that you aren't. It goes without saying that when you lose your job it affects those who are close to you, too. Your spouse, family, friends, boss, and coworkers are all affected by what has happened to you. Unfortunately, the effect on them is often forgotten, and the vital role they play in helping you to move on is sometimes underestimated. Having a support group to help you through the emotional ups and downs is a huge plus in helping you get on your feet and back into the game. Think of them as part of your team. Like any team, each of these individuals plays a different position and has a unique role to fill on the team. Let's look at each of the members on your support team from two perspectives. First, let's explore how they are personally affected by your job loss. Second, let's look at what they can do to help you move forward. Keep in mind that these individuals often do not know what to do or what to say to you after you've been terminated. After all, unless they have been terminated from a job themselves, they don't know or understand what you're experiencing. They want to support you, but they may feel inadequately equipped to do so or may simply not know how to help you. Consequently, they may decide it's best to act as though everything is normal. However, there is a better approach, which usually has to be initiated by you. Let's see what it is.

Spouses and Significant Others

Obviously, your spouse (if you're married) is most affected by your job loss—and in more ways than one. First, as your soulmate, your spouse feels and sees the emotions you experience. After all, unlike the other members of your support team, your spouse lives with you and is with you throughout the entire process: twenty-four hours a day, seven days a week. It's critical that you not take your frustrations out on your spouse. It's not his or her fault that you lost your job. Your spouse will feel your pain and will want to help you more than anyone else will. But your spouse may struggle with knowing how best to help you. It's not an issue of wanting to help, but rather an issue of knowing how to help.

How you can help your spouse help you

1. Talk with your spouse about what you're feeling.

It's important that your spouse understand what you're feeling and thinking as you progress through the grief cycle. All too often we expect our spouses to be able to read our minds, or we assume that he or she knows what we're feeling. The only way your spouse will know what you're feeling or thinking is if you say so. This tends to be easier for women than for men. Women are often more expressive and more ready to share their feelings than men are. Many men like to bottle up their feelings, keeping them private and not letting them show. Some men think it's a sign of weakness to show emotions or feelings—particularly sadness or pain. But it isn't a sign of weakness to show emotions, particularly to those who love you and care the most about you.

2. Ask your spouse to read Chapter Three of this book.

Your spouse will be better equipped to support and help you if he or she understands the emotional roller coaster you will ride after a job loss. Unless you're married to a counselor, a psychologist, or someone who has been professionally trained about the grief cycle, don't expect your spouse to understand and respond appropriately to your feelings. Unless your spouse has lost his or her job in the past, this is a new experience for him or her, too.

3. Make your spouse a partner in the process.

When I got my married, my vows were "for better or for worse." Losing my job certainly wasn't one of the "better" things my wife and I bargained for in our marriage, and I'm sure it wasn't in yours as well. The more you can involve your spouse in helping you cope with your emotions and aid you in finding new work, the quicker you will be able to move forward with your life and career. Remember that your spouse is directly affected by your job loss, too—he or she wants to help you. Shutting out your spouse isn't the solution. The more you can involve your spouse, the better it is for both of you. My wife was a huge help when I lost my job. Sure, she wasn't happy about what happened to me, but she was totally supportive, and her encouragement helped me see the sun on my cloudy days. She was an invaluable resource to me as I weighed my options, and many times she had ideas or made suggestions that I hadn't thought about or had prematurely discounted. She helped me put together my résumé and develop a list of people I needed to network with, as well as making other suggestions that aided me in my career quest. Your spouse can do the same for you if you let him or her help.

4. Discuss your fears and concerns with your spouse.

We don't like to admit that we have fears or concerns, but we all have them. The best way to deal with fears or concerns is to face them head on. Ignoring them will not make them go away. Rick Carson wrote an interesting book, *Taming Your Gremlin: A Surprisingly Simple Method for Getting Out of Your Own Way,* in which he talks about the voices in our heads ("gremlins," as he calls them) that put us down or tell us we can't do something. We often hear those negative voices and obey them. Be aware of your gremlins, who are whispering in your ears ideas such as these:

- You deserved to get fired.
- You'll never find a job as good as the one you lost.
- How are you going to pay those bills now?
- You could never start your own company.
- Who would want to hire you?
- You are a loser.

Don't let your gremlins win the mind game. Admit you have them and discuss them with your spouse. Together, you can slay the little devils or lock them up in a sound-proof cage. Just make sure you face your fears and self-doubts. Only by facing them can you defeat them. The biggest gremlin I faced in thinking about starting my own business was the one I named Doubt. Doubt kept telling me I couldn't be successful working for myself. Where would I get enough clients to make a living? My wife and I talked about Doubt, and I decided to more appropriately rename him Liar. He seldom whispers in my ear today—when he does, I now tune him out.

Pointers for the spouse

If you're the spouse of someone who just lost their job, my heart goes out to you, too. You will probably experience many of the same emotions that your spouse experiences. This is normal and is to be expected. One emotion that many a spouse experiences is anger: not anger at his or her spouse, but at the spouse's boss or company, born out of feelings that his or her spouse didn't deserve to be terminated or wasn't treated fairly in the process. Your reaction is a normal one. However, being angry isn't going to fix the problem or help out your spouse. If both of you are angry and feeding off of each other, it only makes the matter worse. You need to move beyond your anger more quickly so you can help your spouse deal with his or her emotions.

I suggest you read Chapter Three of this book. It will help you understand the emotional roller coaster your spouse is going to go through—and that you, to a lesser extent, will as well—in the days, weeks, and months ahead. Your spouse needs your love, understanding, support, and encouragement as he or she deals with losing a job and seeking new employment. That's why it's so important that you try not to become angry, depressed, or discouraged. This is easier said than done. Your spouse may experience all of these emotions, and when you express the same negative emotions it only adds salt to the wound. Doing this will not help things get better for your spouse. It's important that you be part of the solution along with your spouse, not part of the problem by continually fanning the flames of anger and resentment. If you need to vent your negative feelings, I suggest you do so with someone other than your spouse.

Some dos and don'ts

Here are some dos and don'ts to help you support your spouse as he or she goes through the various stages of the cycle:

Dos

- Do tell your spouse that you're sorry this has happened to him or her. Often a hug and the words "I'm so sorry" are the best things you can give when your spouse is in shock (the denial stage) about what has happened.
- Do give your spouse time to grieve his or her job loss.
- Do ask your spouse to share his or her feelings with you. Periodically ask him or her, "What are you feeling now? Where are you in your thought process?"
- Do be a good listener.
- Do empathize with your spouse.
- Do encourage your spouse throughout the process.
- Do help your spouse get professional help if he or she becomes severely depressed.
- Do consider how you can help with finances.
- Do take an active role in helping with your spouse's job search.
- Do be honest with your spouse and help him or her face reality if necessary.

Don'ts

- Don't say that you know what you're spouse is feeling unless you've lost your job in the past.
- Don't fuel the negative emotions your spouse is feeling.
- Don't pretend that nothing has happened or changed.
- Don't say, "It's only a job—things could be worse." It *is* only a job, but many men, in particular, use jobs as one of the ways they measure their self-worth.
- Don't ignore reality.

Dealing with Finances

Finances are usually a concern after a spouse loses a job, particularly if the spouse who has been terminated was the breadwinner. Financial pressures can add to the stress and emotions both of you are experiencing. You should sit down with your spouse—and with your children if they are teenagers—to candidly discuss your financial situation soon after being terminated. Depending on how much severance you got, as well as how much money you have saved or invested, you may have to make some minor or major adjustments in spending patterns. In some cases, the spouse who wasn't fired may want, or be forced, to find a job to temporarily (or even permanently) help with finances.

When evaluating your financial situation, there are several steps you should consider taking.

1. **Develop a household budget.** If you don't have a budget, you should develop one by identifying all your current expenses. Your expenses typically fall into two categories: fixed and variable expenses. Fixed expenses don't change from month to month. They include items such as rent or mortgage payments, car and life insurance, health care premiums, and cable services. Variable expenses change from month to month and include utilities, food, entertainment, gasoline, clothes, taxes, savings, car maintenance, medical and dental care, household supplies, books and magazines, and dining out. Develop a worksheet on which to list your expenses and income for at least the next six months. Income can include unemployment, sever-

ance, or other income. Once you've filled out your work-sheet, subtract your monthly expenses from your monthly income to discover your balance, which will be either a surplus or deficit.

2. **Adjust your expenses.** After calculating your monthly balance, decide what expenses you can reduce or eliminate completely, at least until you find another job. Although it is sometimes difficult to reduce fixed expenses, many variable expenses can be reduced or eliminated altogether.

3. **Identify your sources of income.** Look at all your sources of income to determine what your income stream will be each month. Sources of income can include unemployment compensation, severance payments, your spouse's income, savings, a 401(k) loan or emergency withdrawal, dividend payments, stock or mutual fund proceeds, home equity, the proceeds of sold assets, and the cash value of insurance policies.

4. **Negotiate with creditors.** Make a list of all your creditors and how much you owe each one of them, including interest rates, monthly payment schedules, and any other helpful information. It takes courage to approach your creditors to ask for their help and understanding. However, it's better to approach them for help than to be unable to make your payments. You may find that many of your

creditors are willing to work with you to develop a mutually agreeable plan for repaying your debts. If you can't make the full payment each month, try to make a partial payment to lower your overall balance and to demonstrate good faith in your repayment of your obligations.

5. **Include your family in the process.** If your children are teenagers or older, include them in the discussion of your financial situation. They must fully understand the situation and be a part of the solution. They will have suggestions and ideas about how to adjust your expenses, including some of their own. Depending on their ages, they may need to find part-time jobs to help with finances until you get back on your feet.

6. **Your spouse may need to take a job.** If your spouse doesn't work outside the home, he or she should consider taking a part-time or full-time job to help bring in additional income. This may be a temporary situation, but any additional income is helpful while you're unemployed.

7. **Check your progress.** Meet at least monthly with your family to discuss and review your budget. These meetings are a good way to get everyone engaged in the process and up to date on the family's financial situation. It's also a good time to make minor tweaks to the budget.

Family

Just like your spouse, your family is directly affected, to varying degrees, by your job loss. If you have older children at home or in college, they will be concerned about you, but they will be also nervous about how your job loss might affect them. If they aren't adults yet, you really can't expect them to understand the emotions you're experiencing. It's not that they don't care about you—they simply can't relate to what you're experiencing. If they are older teenagers, they may not immediately express their concern about possibly having to relocate to another city, leaving their friends. Moving to a new location and school creates stress and uncertainty in most teenagers. If your children are in college and you're funding their education, they will naturally worry about whether or not they will be able to continue their college education. It's important to recognize the concerns your children have and to discuss them openly and honestly with them. You may not have all the answers to their questions, but talking with them will allay many of their concerns and fears. It will also help them better understand what you're going through and how they can best support you. Going through struggles together often proves to be a great bonding experience for families and serves to strengthen family ties.

Your parents, and any siblings you may have, will be concerned about you and will want to help as best they can. Be sure to tell them about what has happened to you and to ask for their support.

> *But there is a friend who stays closer than a brother.*
>
> PROVERBS 18:24

Pointers for teenage and college-aged children

If your parent has just lost their job, you are an important part of his or her support system. You have every right to be concerned about how your parent's job loss might affect you directly, particularly if a new job may be in another city, requiring your family to relocate. As you support your parent, keep these things in mind:

Dos
- Do be supportive and helpful.
- Do talk to your parents about your concerns and fears.
- Do understand that this is a stressful and difficult time for your parents.
- Do understand that your parents are concerned about finances and see what you can do to help them.
- Do consider taking a part-time job to help with finances if necessary.

Don'ts
- Don't be afraid to talk to your parent about what has happened.
- Don't immediately ask if you're going to have to relocate to another city.
- Don't blame your parent if you do have to relocate.
- Don't be negative and increase the stress your parents are already experiencing.

Friends

Your friends can help support you after you lose your job. There is a good chance that one of your friends has lost a job at some point in his or her career. If so, your friend can fully appreciate what you're going through and can offer valuable advice to assist you in finding other employment. Friends who have been down the job-loss road before you can tell you about the bumps, curves, hills, and valleys they traveled after losing their job. Make time to talk to such friends to learn about their feelings, experiences, successes, and failures during their own periods of unemployment. You can learn from their knowledge and experiences, applying them to your own situation.

Friends who haven't lost a job can't fully appreciate your situation or offer first-hand advice, but they are still important allies in your job search. These friends will want to help you, but remember that they don't know exactly what you're feeling or experiencing. They don't want to say the wrong thing to you, so they may not say much of anything about you being terminated when they first see you. They may not even know you lost your job. It's often best if you take the initiative when you see them, explaining what has happened and asking for their support and help. Here is a good way to approach a friend (let's pretend her name is Kim):

You: "Kim, I wanted to let you know that I lost my job last week."

Kim: "You're kidding me, aren't you?"

You: "I wish I were, but I'm not. My company decided to reorganize and downsize, and my job was eliminated in the process. It caught me by surprise. I never thought I would lose my job, but I have, and it's a tough thing to deal with, to be honest with you."

Kim: "How are your husband and kids taking this?"

You: "They were as shocked as I was when it happened. None of us can make sense of it, but they have been very supportive and encouraging. It was tough going home and telling them what happened. I was upset, embarrassed, and confused."

Kim: "What are you going to do?"

You: "I don't know yet, and I haven't given it much

thought at this point. I just don't feel like looking for a new job just yet. I don't think I'm emotionally or mentally prepared at this point."

Kim: "Wow, how can I help you? If I hear of anything that's a good job fit for you, I will let you know."

You: "Thanks—I really appreciate it. It's not been easy, and I'm having some pretty tough struggles."

Kim: "What kind of struggles?"

You: "It's been tough on me emotionally, but talking about it helps me deal with it. I'm glad you've never had to go through this, and I hope you never do. It's not any fun. I've been told that losing a job can be very stressful, and I'm finding out how true that is. At first I was in shock when my boss told me—I stayed that way for most of the next day. A book I'm reading says shock is a normal reaction, the first of five stages I will probably go through, starting with denial and followed by anger, depression, bargaining, and finally acceptance. It must be true, because, to be honest, the last day or two, I've been angry at what happened to me. It doesn't seem fair, but I can't do anything about that."

Kim: "It's *not* fair."

You: "I appreciate your friendship. Right now the best thing you can do for me is to encourage me and be there for me when I need a shoulder to lean on. If you see me stuck in a pity party, a good old fashioned kick in the butt might be in order."

Kim: "You can count on me, as always, but I'm not sure about the kick thing."

You: "I knew I could. It would be helpful if I could use you as a sounding board. Of course, as you mentioned earlier, if you hear of any interesting job leads, please let me know. I'm told most people find jobs through their network of friends and acquaintances."

Your friends do want to help you, but they can support you better if you are honest with them, telling them how they can help you best. No one wants to guess, so don't make them.

Pointers for friends

Here are some dos and don'ts you can share with your friends to let them know how to help you:

Dos
- Do look for opportunities to encourage your friend.
- Do ask what you can do to help.
- Do periodically ask your friend, "What are you struggling with? What are your fears or concerns right now?"
- Do pass along job leads.
- Do help your friend as he or she starts networking.

Don'ts
- Don't say you know what your friend is feeling unless you have lost a job in the past.
- Don't assume that your friend is doing fine emotionally. He or she may be struggling or hurting, and you may not realize it.
- Don't be negative when trying to help your friend.

Coworkers

Your coworkers who didn't lose their jobs are in an awkward position. On one hand, they are happy they didn't get terminated. On the other, they are sad that you lost your job. In fact, many coworkers go through emotional struggles of their own when a friend or coworker is terminated and they aren't. Some counselors refer to it as the survivor syndrome. They are sad and upset to see you lose your job and may actually feel guilty that they didn't lose theirs. They may begin to worry—they survived the axe this time, but they may wonder whether they might not the next time it falls. Some of your coworkers may think you're mad at them because you lost your job and they didn't. This fear could cause some of them not to reach out to you after you leave. In their own minds, they aren't sure how you will react to them, and they don't know what to say to you. It is a difficult and confusing time for them as well. Consequently, they may choose to say nothing rather than risk saying the wrong thing. Don't be surprised if you don't hear from most of your coworkers after you leave the company. My advice to you is to reach out to them first. In doing so, you can let them know you're glad they didn't lose their jobs as well, and that you wish them the best. Maintaining these relationships could be helpful to you as you seek new employment.

This was one of my biggest adjustments when I left my company. There were a number of coworkers I thought I would hear from, but I never did—not a single phone call, e-mail, or text message. To me, this hurt more than losing my job. Surprisingly, I did hear from some coworkers who I never thought would contact me after I left. I appreciate their reaching out to me even if only to let me know they were thinking of me.

Pointers for coworkers

After one of your coworkers loses his or her job, don't ignore him or her or pretend that it didn't happen. People who just lost their jobs are going to struggle emotionally not only with being let go but also with losing the camaraderie and pleasure of working with you and their other coworkers. I encourage you to reach out to them, because this simple act of caring really helps bolster their spirits. You may be concerned that you don't know what to say or that you will say the wrong thing. The best words you can say are simply, "I'm so sorry you lost your job. What can I do to help you?" This is all you need to say—it's the thing your coworkers most need to hear.

Dos

- Do stay in touch with your coworker as he or she looks for other work. You can call, leave a voice-mail, or send an e-mail or text message, even if simply to say that he or she is in your thoughts or to check in on how things are going.
- Do reach out to your coworker who has been fired.
- Do say you're sorry about what happened to him or her.
- Do listen more than you talk.
- Do let your coworker vent to you.
- Do offer to help your coworker if you can.
- Do be an encourager.
- Do pass along any job prospects you hear about.

Don'ts

- Don't fear contacting your coworker after he or she has been terminated.
- Don't tell them you know how they're feeling unless you've lost a job in the past.
- Don't be critical of your company for firing your coworker.
- Don't talk too much.

It helps you to try to see things through the eyes of your family, friends, and coworkers. What's happened to you affects them too, and they have their own set of emotions and issues to process. Reach out to them and ask them for their help if you know that they will be a positive, not negative, influence as you move forward.

There are two types of people in the world: adders and subtractors. Adders enrich your life and make you a better person. They encourage you and bring out the best in you. They have a positive view of life, and you feel energized when you're around them. Subtractors pull you down and bring out the worst in you. They want to pull you down to their level with their words and actions. They have a negative view of life, and you feel drained when you're around them. Don't have any subtractors as part of your support system. Avoid them at all costs. It's a difficult time for you, and surrounding yourself with adders will lift your spirits and give you hope. I'm thankful for the many adders I had in my life when I lost my job.

You should step back for a moment and realize that you, too, are either an adder or subtractor. Sure—after getting fired, it's easy to find yourself in the subtractor camp. But if you do find yourself there, make sure you're a visitor just passing through. Don't stop at this camp, set up your tent, and make it home. Move through this camp quickly and head for the adder camp.

It's now time to focus our energy and effort on finding that new job or career. We need to target our thinking in order to accelerate our results. You've come through the worst part of the storm: look up and you'll see the blue skies on the horizon.

Kent's Story

Until December 2005, I worked nine years for a large power company, managing their California energy assets. Like many energy companies in the country, we had gotten involved in energy trading and found ourselves facing some serious financial difficulties as a result. In November 2005, I was told we would be selling some businesses, consolidating others, and laying off people. A few weeks later, I was given the option of taking a lateral job in another state or severance. I wrestled with what to do, particularly taking the severance and facing the unknown. After talking with my wife and family, we decided that we didn't want to transfer and chose to take the severance offer instead. It wasn't an easy decision, but we felt it was the right one for us. I wanted to take a couple of months off after being released to decompress and unwind.

I was offered outplacement by my company, and I

decided to take advantage of the offer. I went to outplacement and decided to hit the search process hard so that I could find a job quickly. I anticipated that I would be able to find another job quickly, but it didn't go as quickly as I thought it would. I started working through my network list as I was coached to do. I had never prepared a network list of friends and associates in my circle of influence, and it ended up a smaller list than I had anticipated. Once I had worked through my list, I struggled with calling back people on my list as the outplacement counselors urged me to do. I felt self-conscious calling people back; to me it was like cold-calling, something I didn't feel comfortable doing. It was definitely outside my comfort zone, making it difficult for me to stay engaged in the networking process. I forced myself to do it, and I ended up finding a job in about six months through someone I had known at my former company. Networking wasn't easy for me to do, but it is a critical step in finding another job. After a few months of not getting any offers, I was starting to get somewhat anxious and second-guessing my decision to turn down the transfer and take the severance offer. The emotion I struggled with most was self-doubt. At times, I felt like I was wandering in the desert and wondered if I had made the right decision.

I did find another job in about six months through my

network; in my case it was a lead given to me by an employee I had worked with at my former employer. I do encourage those who lose jobs to take the time to step back and think about their values and priorities. It's a great opportunity to re-evaluate your life and to decide what you want to do with the rest of it.

One of my biggest surprises and disappointments was the number of associates I telephoned to network with who never bothered to return my phone calls. Having been through the experience of losing a job, I'm much more empathetic and sensitive to people going through job loss. I have now made it a priority to return their calls and to try to help them if I can.

PART TWO

MOVING FORWARD

CHAPTER FIVE

Change Is Inevitable

For every evil under the sun,
There be a remedy or there be none;
Is there's one, try to find it,
Is there's none, then never mind it.

WILLIAM DEAN HAWKINS, MEDAL OF HONOR RECIPIENT

Y ou climb into your automobile, shut your door, and buckle your seatbelt. As soon as you turn the ignition, the engine roars to life and you shift the transmission into drive. You fix your eyes on the rearview mirror as you step on the accelerator and start down the street. After going only a few feet, you hear a loud crash and are jolted to a hard stop as your air bag deploys. You quickly realize you must have run into something, but you're not sure what you hit—after all, you were looking in the rearview mirror. You put the car into park, turn off the engine, push the air bag away from your face, and, after unlocking your seat-belt, open the door and get out of the car. You immediately notice that you've run into the rear of a car parked on the side of the street. You think, *It's not easy driving forward while only looking at my rearview mirror.*

Letting Go of the Past

You're probably thinking to yourself as you read this, "David, no one drives their car forward while looking into their rearview mirror." You're correct. It would be stupid, dangerous, and potentially deadly to drive in this fashion. Yet, how many people have you met who are trying to live while focusing on the rearview mirror of their life? These people seem obsessed with the past. They seem to always be focused on the past. It could be that in the past they found themselves in a comfort zone they didn't want to leave. That comfort zone became their security blanket. They might have made some mistakes in their past and might be continually mentally and emotionally reliving them by thinking about missed opportunities, poor decisions, and failed relationships. I've known several people who fit this description, and I'll bet you do, too.

The past is over. You certainly want to remember the fond memories you have of the past, but don't dwell on the negative ones. Nothing you can do will change the past. It's like a canceled check. Now that it's been cashed, it is of no use to anyone.

> *Yesterday is history. Tomorrow is a mystery. Today is a gift— that's why it's called "the present."*

What a powerful quote! Yesterday is history. All you can do is learn from it. Look at what happened in the past: learn something helpful from it and do things differently today. You and I have no control over tomorrow—or even a guarantee we will live to see tomorrow. It is a mystery. But we need to plan for tomorrow so that if it does come, we will be ready to make the most of it.

The only thing we do have is today. It's truly a present that we can unwrap and use in any way we desire. It's up to us to decide what we will do with our day. Will we make the most of each opportunity, or will we waste it on unproductive and unimportant things? Time is a precious commodity. When we waste time, we waste our lives. I've always admired Pat Williams, executive vice president of the Orlando Magic. Pat knows how to make the most of his time. He has written over forty books, given hundreds of speeches across the country, run in over forty-nine marathons, and teaches a weekly Sunday school class, all while raising nineteen children, fourteen of whom are adopted. I'm amazed at how much he accomplishes with everything he has on his plate each day. In one of Pat's books, *Go for the Magic,* he talks about the value of time.

How will you spend your time?

He says in the book:

Someone once made this analogy: Suppose your bank made you a special offer. It will put $86,400 in your account every single morning, and it's all yours to use exactly as you see fit on anything you wish. There's only one catch. Whatever you fail to spend by the end of the day, the bank will take back. The next day, same deal: $86,400 in your account to use as you want—but the bank keeps the unspent surplus. What would you do with that bank account? You know what you'd do! You'd go to the bank first thing every morning and draw every nickel from that account. Well, the amazing truth is that this deal has already been made to you. There's an account with your name on it, only instead of dollars, it's filled with seconds—86,400 seconds. At the start of every day, you have 86,400 seconds. You can spend those seconds any way you want to. (Williams 1995, 30)

Once again, we have a choice. We get the privilege of deciding every single day how we're going to spend our

86,400 seconds. We can use them for work, sleep, play, exercise, reading, talking, thinking—the list is endless. I often hear people complain they don't have enough time to get anything done. Yet, they have the same 86,400 seconds deposited into their time account each day that you and I have. But do they use it wisely? Do they spend their time doing the important things, or only the urgent things in their lives? How about you?

> *Time is what we want most, but . . . what we use worst.*
>
> WILLIAM PENN

Are you using your time wisely? How are you spending your 86,400 seconds each day? I don't know how you're spending them, but I do know that you're spending them on something. That's why managing your time every single day is so important. If you don't control it, someone will control it for you. Other people will control your time by forcing you to fit it into their schedules. Before long, you will discover that other people, not you, are controlling your destiny. Each of those 86,400 seconds is used on an event. An event can be anything from sleeping to sitting at a stop light. Our lives are simply the summation of the hundreds of events in each of our days. Here is a powerful secret: control your events, control your life. What you and I do today determines who we become in the future. Why? The secret of our future is hidden in our daily agenda and in the events that compose it.

Author and leadership expert John Maxwell expands on this secret in his book *Today Matters*. Maxwell says,

It all comes down to what you do today. When I talk about your daily 'agenda,' I don't mean your to-do list. Nor am I asking you to adopt a particular kind of calendar or computer program to manage your time. I'm focusing on something bigger. I want you to embrace what may be a whole new approach to life. Make the decision once, and then manage it daily. There are only a handful of important decisions people need to make in their entire lifetimes. Does that surprise you? Most people complicate life and get bogged down in decision making. My goal has always been to make things as simple as possible. I've boiled the big decisions down to twelve things. Once I've made those decisions, all I have to do is manage how I'll follow through on them. If you make decisions in those key areas once and for all—and then manage those decisions daily—you can create the kind of tomorrow you desire. Successful people make right decisions early, and manage those decisions daily. (Maxwell 2004, 14–15)

Does it sound too simple? It's not as complicated as you might think. You need to decide what's important in your life—what you truly value. By determining what you value, you can manage your agenda to reflect those values. As Maxwell says, you only need to make those decisions once and then manage them daily. The result is that you're managing the activities of your life and making sure your activities are in alignment with your values. By doing so, you're not only managing your time wisely but also managing your life. Don't think of it as time management; think of it as *life management—living with purpose.* We will explore purpose and values in more detail in the next chapter.

Learn to Embrace Change

Do you like change in your life? Most of us, if we're honest with ourselves, do not like change. We are creatures of habit, and we like to stay in our self-created comfort zones. In losing your job, you're undergoing a major change. You no longer have a workplace to go to. You probably had a routine you followed each day: when you left the house, the route you took to work and home each evening, how you organized your workflow, and when and where you went to lunch. You had structure in your life, much of it revolving around your job, because that is where you spent the majority of your time each day. All of that has changed. It was a change you had no choice over.

Why do we resist change in our lives? I think there are a number of reasons:

- Change is sometimes **disconcerting**.
- Change is sometimes **uncomfortable**.
- Change is sometimes **negative**.
- Change is sometimes **disruptive**.
- Change is sometimes **painful**.
- Change is sometimes **unnecessary**.

Change is sometimes one or all of these things. We all have experienced some changes in our lives that we didn't like.

It's human nature to move towards pleasure and away from pain. Ed Foreman, a motivational speaker, said that we will not change until the pain of change is less than the pain of staying the same.

We love doing things that bring us pleasure. We dislike doing things that bring us pain. All too often we automatically assume that any change we undergo will be for the worse. When we lost our job, we assumed we wouldn't find another job as good as the last one. But often, we find a new job we like much better than the old one. We need to remember some things:

- Change is sometimes **rewarding**.
- Change is sometimes **comfortable**.
- Change is sometimes **positive**.
- Change is sometimes **calming**.
- Change is sometimes **pleasurable**.
- Change is sometimes **necessary**.
- Change is sometimes **the best thing that can happen to us**.

Change is Inevitable

There is no escaping change. We live in a changing world. It seems that the rate of change is growing exponentially—because it is. Much change is driven by technology. The automobiles we drive, the appliances we operate, the watches we wear, and the telephones we talk on—to name only a few things—are much more technologically advanced today than they were even five years ago. We almost need to be engineers to read through some owner's manuals. I bought a stereo receiver as part of a surround system a few weeks ago that came with a 60-page owner's manual. After installing all seven speakers, I worried about how I would balance all of them to make the system sound good. The manual showed a complicated manual technique I could use to balance each speaker. However, as I read the manual, I discovered the system came with an automated balancer. All I had to do was place a small microphone that came with the receiver in the center of the room and instruct the system to auto balance itself. The receiver did so by sending a series of audible tones to each speaker. After hearing the tones from each speaker, the system balanced itself without me doing anything other than unplugging the microphone when I was instructed to do so. In this case, technology simplified my life rather than complicating it.

Our world is going to keep changing faster and faster. I heard a technologist make a presentation recently in which he said, "80 percent of the technology we will be using ten years from now hasn't been invented yet." As a result of these rapid changes, companies and jobs will have to keep changing too. Experts are predicting that the members of Generations X and Y will have as many as ten different careers—not jobs—in their lifetimes. Talk about change! Changes in technology will have a huge effect on how employees work. Employees will have to be constantly learning and training to acquire new skills. Some experts are predicting that within the next ten years, the average worker will spend one week out of every four in training.

CHAPTER SIX

The Dash

Most men lead lives of quiet desperation and go to the grave with the song still in them.

HENRY DAVID THOREAU

I f you go to the cemetery and look at the tombstones, you'll notice they all have something in common. Each tombstone has two dates on it, separated by a short dash. The dates signify the day the person was born and the day the person died. Both dates are but a moment in time: a beginning and an end to an earthly life. The person had no control over either date, unless he or she died by suicide. What the person did have control over was that little innocuous dash between the dates, which now represents his or her life. What do you want your dash to be?

When I was fired, the thought dawned on me that I was

free at that point to do anything I wanted to do with my life. In many ways, it was as though a burden had been lifted from my shoulders. I had an opportunity to start my career over with a blank canvas that I, the artist, could paint any way I liked. I was no longer constrained by my past, but I was the artist of my future. It was up to me to create it; no one was going to do it for me. I now had the opportunity to reinvent myself from a career perspective.

It's true for you, too. What do you want to paint on your canvas? Ultimately, your painting may look a lot like your past painting—or it may look completely different. As the artist of your life, you may never have this opportunity again, so make the most of it. I suspect that you didn't choose to get to this point by being fired. But how you got here really doesn't matter. What does matter is what you are going to do with the rest of your life from today onward.

A Vacation

When my son and daughter were getting ready to graduate from high school, we decided we wanted to take a family vacation to Europe. Several months before the trip, we started exploring travel books of the different countries, looking at pictures and maps on the Internet, and talking with friends who had been to Europe. We sat down with a travel agent and got information and ideas from her about the best tourist sites, hotels, and restaurants, as well as other literature on the history of cities such as London, Rome, Paris, and others. We studied all the information and picked the dates for the trip. Rather than go with a tour group, we decided we wanted to see Europe on our own. We chose the dates for our trip and made our flight reservations. After much discussion, we selected which countries and cities we wanted to visit. We decided to start in London and travel by train to France, Switzerland, Austria, Germany, and Italy before returning to England again. We carefully mapped out which cities we would visit on our 12-day trip and at which hotels we would stay. Our travel agent helped us book the hotels in advance, assuring of of a place to stay each night. Based on our research and planning, we knew which sites and places we wanted to visit in each city upon arriving. Our trip took place before the Euro became the common currency of Europe, so each country had a different currency and we exchanged them almost daily. I carefully prepared an envelope for each day of the trip that contained our train tickets, hotel confirmations, currency, and list of sites we planned on seeing. Our family had a great time, and it is our favorite

> *If you aim at nothing, you'll hit it every time.*
>
> ANONYMOUS

vacation to date. The vacation was a success largely because we had carefully planned it and knew what we wanted to do each day. We knew where we wanted to go, what we wanted to do, and when we wanted to do it.

Like us, most people carefully plan their vacations and trips. They put a lot of thought into making sure that they get to each of their planned destinations and have a good time each day. It's sad but true that most people spend more time planning their vacations than they do their lives. They take the time and make the effort to plan their vacation, but they wander through life without any purpose, bereft of goals.

Then they wonder why their lives fell short of their expectations and dreams. Some people struggle with letting go of their past and embracing the change that is necessary to move forward, but you don't have to be one of them.

The Power of Purpose

I believe God created each of us for a distinct purpose. Not only did He create us for a purpose, He gave us the gifts and abilities to achieve our purpose. Living with purpose is the secret to success and happiness. Everything that God created He created for a specific purpose. He created man and woman to take care of His creation and to have a personal relationship with Him. Everything

He created—the sun, moon, stars, water, animals, birds, insects, and much, much more—is for a unique purpose. Everything man makes is for a purpose: vehicles to transport people or goods from one place to another, telephones to communicate with each other, clothes to keep us warm or cool, electricity to light our buildings and streets. Every living or created thing has a purpose. You and I are no different. We often struggle to find our real purpose in life, but when we do find our purpose, life takes on new meaning.

In his book *In Pursuit of Purpose,* Dr. Myles Munroe says, "Until purpose is discovered, existence has no meaning, for purpose is the source of fulfillment." He says that purpose is many things (Munroe 1992):

- the original intent for the creation of a thing
- the original reason for the existence of a thing
- the end for which the means exist
- the cause for the creation of a thing
- the desired result that initiates production
- the need that makes a manufacturer produce a specific product
- the destination that prompts the journey
- the expectation of the source
- the objective for the subject
- the aspiration for the inspiration
- the object one wills or resolves to have

Purpose, therefore, must come before something is created or made. Purpose determines production, not production determines purpose. Purpose begins with the end in mind. It answers the simple but profound question: *Why* does something exist? When you and I answer the *why* question to our lives, the *what*, *when*, *how*, and *where* questions become much clearer. But people too often focus on the latter questions only, completely ignoring the former.

As you begin your search for a job, take the time to think about your unique purpose. I hope your last job was aligned with your purpose. If it wasn't, you now have the opportunity to find a job or career that helps fulfill your purpose. You might be thinking, "I would like to do such and such a thing, but I have bills coming due, and I get no, or very little, severance pay. I have to find another job quickly. I don't have the time to think about purpose; I'm worried about surviving." You're right; our first instinct is to survive. And survival may mean taking a temporary job— perhaps the first job that comes along. If this is what you must do, then by all means, do it. But that doesn't mean that you have to continue doing this for the rest of your working life. Because much of the immediate pressure will be lifted after finding work, you have the opportunity to focus on discovering and fulfilling your purpose. When you do, you can quit the job you took out of necessity to take a job that aligns with your purpose. Don't get caught up in the comfort zone of simply having a job, settling for doing

> *Pursue your passion, not your paycheck.*

something that you have little, if any passion, for doing. Sure, it's a paycheck and benefit package, but I hope you aren't willing to go through the motions each day—for an entire lifetime—to settle for a paycheck.

He is considered one of the greatest conquerors and military leaders the world has ever known. He never lost a battle, and by the time of his death at the age of thirty-three, he had conquered most of the known world. He was driven by his dreams and goals. Men wanted to be led by him; women wanted to be loved by him. With each victory and conquest, his fame and legend grew. He achieved fame, wealth, and success. History records that after he had conquered the known world, he sat down, placed his head in his hands, and wept. He had achieved all his goals and had nothing else to look forward to. Historians believe that at that point, he became despondent, his drinking worsening until his death a few years later. Alexander the Great lived for his goals. The story of Alexander proves that achieving goals and finding success alone is not enough.

The Station

Robert J. Hastings wrote a short story called "The Station." The story is about a vision many of us share. In his story, we're on a long train trip looking out the window taking in the splendor of the world as it passes by. But we're constantly thinking about our final destination and the day we finally arrive at our station. We will be greeted by bands playing and flags waving. All of our dreams will then come true; our lives will take on new meaning. But until then we pace the aisles counting the slowly passing minutes, always thinking about arriving at the station.

Hastings points out that at some point, we realize that there is no one station, no one place that we will arrive at once and for all. It's a dream, and it constantly outdistances us. We continually reach for it, but we never quite get there. For many, it means, "I will be happy and successful *one day.*" That one day can be reaching a certain age, getting married, becoming the vice president at work, having kids, paying off the mortgage, or retiring. Sadly, once we get there, it disappears. As Hastings says, "the station somehow hides itself at the end of an endless track." He admonishes us to live in the moment—to stop pacing the aisles waiting for our station to arrive.

What is your station? Is it a nicer car, a bigger house, or more money in the bank? Do you ever say, "When I get that promotion, I will . . ." or "When the kids are grown, we will . . ." or "When we start drawing our pension, we will . . ."? If you have, you're on the train looking for your station. A lot of people have made material things their station:

- A man who was head of one of the world's largest monopolies
- A man who was one of the most successful speculators on Wall Street
- The former president of the largest independent steel company in American
- A past chairman of one of the country's largest utility companies
- A former president of the largest gas company in the United States
- A man who was once president of the Bank of International Settlements
- A man who was a member of President Harding's cabinet

What happened to all of these individuals after enduring the Great Depression?

- Ivar Krueger, head of International Match Corporation, known as the "match king," died of suicide or was murdered. The truth was never discovered.
- Jesse Livermore, the "most wondrous of the 'boy wonders' of Wall Street," died of suicide.
- Charles M. Schwab, chairman of Bethlehem Steel, died penniless.

- Samuel Insull, chairman of Commonwealth Edison Company and other utility corporations, was acquitted on embezzlement and mail-fraud charges. He died in Paris in modest surroundings.
- Howard Hopson, president of the Associated Gas and Electric Utility empire, went to prison for mail fraud and died in a sanitarium.
- Leon Fraser, president of the World Bank for International Settlements, died of suicide.
- Albert Fall, Harding's Secretary of the Interior, served prison time for accepting a bribe.

Sooner or later we learn that there is no station in this life. It's not about the destination; it's about the journey and the experiences we encounter on the way. I've met a lot of people who lived to work. Their life revolved around their jobs and careers. Few of them had any interests or hobbies outside of work. Several of them told me they were looking forward to retirement, when they could finally enjoy life, spend time with their families, and find some fun hobbies. I've discovered that these people have the most difficult time when they do finally retire. It's a difficult transition for them. If you don't have interests outside of your current job, you probably will not begin to have them when you retire.

> *When a man does not know what harbor he is making for, no wind is the right wind.*
>
> SENECA

Develop hobbies and interests now that will carry through into your retirement years.

Wylie was a good leader and highly respected within the company he worked for. He had worked there for almost forty years and had risen to a key position in the company through hard work and dedication. The company was the most important thing in his life. He had put aside a considerable sum of money for his retirement in addition to having a very comfortable pension. I was talking to Wylie a few years before he retired and was asking him what he was going to do when that time came. He told me about all the things he wanted to do: hobbies he wanted to start and places he wanted to go, none of which he had started doing while he was working. When Wylie did finally retire, he had a difficult time adjusting to not having a job. He never started the new hobbies or visited the places he talked about. Within one year of retirement, Wylie died, a wealthy man who never got to his station.

> *Some people wonder why their lives never change or get better, yet they keep thinking and behaving in the same way they always have.*

Now, not someday, is the time to start living. Don't get into a rut. A rut is nothing more than a grave with both ends kicked out. It's easy to get into a rut. Here are some symptoms of rut-living:

- Working for a paycheck only
- Following the same set of routines day after day
- Disliking any change in your life
- Thinking, *If it's not broken, don't fix it*
- Believing that learning stopped when you graduated from school
- Getting frustrated when someone new sits in your seat at church
- Eating the same foods all the time
- Saying to yourself, *We've always done it this way*

If you have several of the symptoms just mentioned, there's a good chance you're in a rut. You're in a rut for one simple reason—because you choose to be. The good news is that you can choose to get out of the rut. But choice alone will not pull you out of the rut.

The only way out is to take action. You can't change your life without first changing your thoughts and then your actions. You will never leave where you are until you decide where you want to be and then start mov-

If you always do what you have always done, you will always get what you always got.

ing in that direction. If the job you just got fired from was a rut, you should be jumping up and down with joy. Now you can start over and find a job that makes you excited about going to work each day. It's an opportunity to work with new people and learn new things.

I love being around people who love life. I find that they embrace change, enjoy challenges, and make the best of everything that life throws at them. It doesn't matter whether life throws them a fast ball, curve ball, or sinker: they stand in the batter's box and keep swinging. Even the occasional bean ball doesn't keep them down. They simply hit the ground and jump back up, ready for the next pitch. They love life. My late friend Mike Duffy was a great example of this type of person.

> Life is not a journey to the grave with intention of arriving in a pretty and well-pressed body, but rather to skid in broadside, thoroughly used up, totally worn out and loudly proclaiming . . . "Wow, what a ride!".

Mike was full of energy, passion, and purpose. He loved his job, and he enjoyed the people he encountered every day. I never saw Mike in a rut; he was always dreaming and thinking about what could be, not what was. Whenever I saw Mike, I could bet that there would be a smile on his face. Mike wasn't just an adder, he was a multiplier. He made you believe you could do anything. Whenever he ended a meeting or conversation with someone, he always said, "life is good"—and to him it was. Ironically, a few months before Mike died from a heart attack, he sent me the following quote: "Life is not a journey to the grave with intention of arriving in a pretty and well-pressed body, but rather to skid in broadside, thoroughly used up, totally worn out and loudly proclaiming . . . "Wow, what a ride!"

Mike lived that kind of life. You can too, but only when you discover your purpose.

How to Discover Your Life Purpose

Purpose answers the critically important question: "Why do you exist?" All of us exist for a specific purpose. Otherwise, life has little meaning. We are just going through the motions day after day, simply passing time. Discovering our purpose frees us to experience all areas of our life at a much higher and more fulfilling level. I think there are a number of clues to help us discover our life purpose. Let's take a closer look at them.

What are your unique talents and abilities?

I believe everyone has certain innate talents, things they are naturally good at doing. When someone is naturally talented at something, it seems to come easily to him or her. I know many people who can sing beautifully or who find it easy to learn to play a musical instrument. They are talented or gifted musically, sensitive to pitch, tone, and rhythm. Others may have the ability to draw, paint, or design things. These people think spatially and make great artists, graphic designers, and architects. Some people are natural athletes and excel in sports or in activities requiring physical agility. We watch in awe as they fly through the air and do a 360-degree dunk holding a basketball, catch a football running at full speed, or drive a golf ball 300-plus yards into the middle of the fairway. I'm amazed at people who are talented mathematically. They are able to solve complex technical problems, design sophisticated machines, and create new products.

Even someone who doesn't possess an innate talent or ability can still learn to play a musical instrument, paint a picture, or catch a football. A person can become competent at many of these things with enough hard work and practice. But even if you do learn to do these things, you most likely won't be as good at it as someone who is naturally talented in those same things. You may enjoy playing basketball, but if you're five feet tall, you'll never dunk a basketball without the help of a trampoline.

Some people may not be able to do certain things well no matter how hard they work or practice. I'm a prime example. I would love to be able to sing, but I can't carry a tune, of which I'm often reminded by my family and friends whenever I sing. No amount of hard work or practice will make me into a singer. On the other hand, I do have the natural ability to draw and design things. In my mind's eye, I've always been able to see compositions and to realize what would look good on a canvas or sketch. I love photography and take thousands of pictures each year. I can look at a landscape or scene and immediately frame in my mind's eye what part of the scene would look good in a photograph and what part should be excluded.

You have a set of unique talents and abilities. Take some time to think through your unique talents and abilities. Below, list two or three of them that will best serve you as you move forward with your new job or career.

1.

2.

3.

What are your unique skills?

Just as you have innate talents and abilities, you also have skills and experiences of which you can take advantage. Skills are things we have learned or acquired through study, training, and practice. If you're a craftsperson, you have a set of unique skills. Perhaps you're an electrician, plumber, carpenter, or bricklayer. You may be technically trained with unique skills in areas such as automation, interior design, health care, computers, or other technical fields. As a businessperson, your unique skill sets give you the ability to communicate orally or verbally, to analyze data, solve unique and difficult problems, program computers, perform laboratory tests, teach or train others, program computers, develop marketing or advertising programs, or prepare financial reports.

We have learned skills by attending college, technical schools, educational classes, or the school of hard knocks. I suspect that all of us have gone through numerous training programs designed to equip us with different skill sets for use in our jobs or careers. I can recall programs to which my company sent me during my career to provide me with skills in the areas of managing others, interviewing, conducting performance discussions, making effective presentations, improving employee safety, conducting root cause analyses, coaching employees, and managing time—or to improve those skills I already had.

Think about the various training you've received in the past. Much or all of it may transfer into your next job or career.

Below, make a list of the skills you've acquired that are

the most beneficial to you:

1.

2.

3.

4.

5.

6.

You may be surprised at how many skills you've acquired up to this point of your job or career.

What are your unique educational and life experiences?

All of us have varying levels of education. Some of you may not have graduated from high school or college. Others may have a degree from a technical school or another type of specialized school. Some of you may have done postgraduate work or obtained special certifications. Many people continue attending special continuing education classes while working in order to maintain their licenses or certifications. Regardless of how little or how much education you may have, the education you do have, coupled with your unique skills, can be used as a springboard to help you find your next job or to launch you into a totally new career. To borrow from the Visa commercial: your education is "priceless." Take advantage of it and put it to work for you.

> *It's what you know after you learn it all that counts.*
>
> JOHN WOODEN, FORMER UCLA HEAD BASKETBALL COACH

But be careful not to use your knowledge as a crutch or to let it limit you. You may say, "David, I was educated in college as an accountant and passed my CPA exam. Shouldn't I be an accountant for the rest of my career?" I can't answer that question for you: only you can. What I *can* tell you is that your training and years of experience as an accountant do not obligate you to always be an accountant. I know a number of trained professionals—accountants, lawyers, doctors, teachers—who made complete career changes. One of them is running a bed and breakfast, another has opened a restaurant, and another became a writer. They decided to make major career changes to pursue their passions. Some of them aren't making as much money as they did previously, but they are much happier and more fulfilled, because their careers are aligned with their life purposes.

Some NASCAR races require cars to use a restrictor plate that restricts the amount of air taken into the carburetor, thereby limiting the car's horsepower and speed. Don't let your education or lack of it become a restrictor plate in your life. If you do, it will limit how fast and how far you can go.

Your skills are used daily in doing your job. We use skills so much that we often take them for granted or even forget that we have them. We apply our skills routinely to help us meet the objectives and accomplish the tasks associated with our jobs. As a result of applying these skills in our work environment, we have experiences that help us grow professionally. It's nothing more than applying the things we've been taught and trained to do in order to accomplish our jobs. All of these experiences teach us valuable lessons.

> *Experience is not what happens to a man. It is what a man does with what happens to him.*
>
> ALDOUS LEONARD HUXLEY

Many of our experiences turn out to be successful. Those successes, whether closing sales, completing projects, making presentations, repairing broken circuits, or winning lawsuits, give us confidence in our abilities. Each small accomplishment and success can lead to larger successes.

But we also experience failures and mistakes. They, too are great teachers, showing us what we need to do better—or not at all. I've learned more valuable lessons about business and life from my failures than I have from my successes. After being fired, it's easy to think you've failed or that you're a failure. I've got great news for you—you're not a failure. Failure is never final or fatal unless you let it be. Losing your job may have felt like a knockout blow or a sucker punch to you that sent you spiraling to the mat. Don't stay down! Get back up on your feet and fight on. Heed the famous words of Winston Churchill spoken in 1941, during one of Britain's darkest moments. "This is the lesson: never give in, never give in, never, never, never, never—in nothing, great or small, large or petty—never give in except to convictions of honour and good sense. Never yield to force; never yield to the apparently overwhelming might of the enemy."

Our History Books Are Filled with Failures

If your résumé had the following points in it like this man's résumé, would you have given up?

- Lost his job
- Defeated for legislature
- Failed in business
- Elected to the legislature
- Sweetheart died
- Suffered nervous breakdown
- Defeated for speaker of the House
- Defeated for nomination for Congress
- Elected to Congress
- Lost renomination
- Rejected for land officer
- Defeated for Senate
- Defeated for nomination for Vice-President
- Again defeated for Senate

This person certainly experienced many failures in his lifetime. Some might even call him a failure, but he certainly wasn't. This is the résumé of Abraham Lincoln before he was elected President of the United States in 1860. Few, if any people, think of Lincoln as a failure; most consider him our greatest president.

Thomas Edison was America's most prolific inventor with 1,093 patents to his name. He had 1,800 prototypes fail before he created the first light bulb. When asked about all the failures, Edison responded, "We now know a thousand ways not to build a light bulb."

Albert Einstein, noble prize winner in physics, was a poor elementary school student. He even failed his first college exam at Zurich Polytechnic. But he went on to develop the theory of relativity and is considered one of the greatest scientists ever to have lived.

Colonel Harland Sanders is the founder of Kentucky Fried Chicken. He dropped out of school at age fourteen and wandered from job to job. At age sixteen, he became a streetcar conductor only to be fired a few weeks later. He tried other jobs before becoming a locomotive fireman for the Southern Railroad, which also fired him. He tried numerous other jobs with no success. At age forty, he opened up a small gas station in rural Kentucky. He added a diner and starting serving food to travelers and local guests. Here he started experimenting with different seasonings to improve the taste of his chicken. He eventually discovered his famous recipe by combining eleven herbs and spices. His chicken became such a hit with travelers and locals that he decided at age sixty-five that he would franchise his recipe and business. The next few years, he traveled around the country trying to sell his recipe and idea. On the 1,009th try, he got his first sale. Today, KFC is a worldwide success.

What is your unique passion?

I find when I get to know someone who begins to open up to me that there are usually one or two things he or she is very passionate about. That passion is like an eternal flame burning inside that never goes out and that, at certain times, roars like a bonfire. The things we are most passionate about are usually those things that most excite us or most break our heart. I find that doing things related to my passions brings me immense joy and excitement. I love doing it and wish it would go on forever.

I have one professional passion and one personal passion. My professional passion is centered on the issue of leadership. I love being around great leaders, seeing how they do things, learning what makes them tick. For years, I've studied the lives of great leaders in history: Abraham Lincoln, Robert E. Lee, U. S. Grant, Jack Welch, Pat Summit, John Wooden, to name a few. In my library, I have hundreds of books on the topic of leadership and leaders. I have hundreds of leadership audio tapes that I listen to, and I have had the privilege of working with some outstanding leaders during my career, as well as the chance to talk one-on-one with some of the gurus of leadership, such as Stephen Covey and John Maxwell.

My personal passion is photography. Put a camera in my hands and throw me in the woods—it doesn't get any better than that. I think the reason I love photography is that it lets me explore the artistic and creative side of my personality. I carry a small digital camera with me everywhere I travel just so that if great photographic opportunity arises, I will be ready to capture it. When I'm on vacation or taking a long trip, I usually drag along all my career gear, which is a backpack-full, including a large tripod. My family has gotten used to me walking around on vacation with a tripod and camera slung over my shoulder. Maybe that's why they started calling me "Captain Tripod." I take from four thousand to five thousand digital pictures each year, and if time permitted, I would easily double that number. You know you're passionate about photography when you stop on an interstate and get on your belly in the median to take a closc-up picture of a flower, or when you get up on a cold snowy day two hours before sunrise and drive forty miles to capture a sunrise over a lake.

> *Follow your passion,*
> *and success will*
> *follow you.*
>
> ARTHUR BUDDHOLD

People may not talk about the things they are passionate about, but watch them long enough and you will discover their passions. Tim's passion is working with at-risk kids who don't have a father. Tim's dad died when he was only eight years old, so for most of his life he didn't have a dad or any father figure in his life. He becomes tearful recalling how much he missed having a dad around to play ball with, talk to, or take him to ball games. Tim is now grown and the father of two teenage children with whom he has a great relationship. But Tim also serves as a foster dad to Matt, a nine-year-old who doesn't have a dad in his life. Matt spends every weekend with Tim and his family. Tim is passionate about helping Matt and about making a difference in his life.

If you look at the lives of people like Abraham Lincoln, Mother Teresa, Martin Luther King, Jr., Jonas Salk, George Washington Carver, and Helen Keller, you'll find that they all had something in common. They all had passions that consumed them to the point of becoming the focuses of their lives. The pursuits of such passions led to their greatness.

What are you passionate about? Find that fire that burns inside of you, and you will find your passion. List your passions below, and think about ways you can possibly propel your passions into your job or career.

1.

2.

3.

What is your unique personality?

You are unique. There is no one else like you. We should be thankful we all are different. Can you imagine how boring the world would be if everyone was alike? Although each of us is unique, many of us do have similar personalities or temperaments. Understanding your temperament, as well as its natural strengths and weaknesses, can help guide you in selecting the right job or career. One type of temperament isn't better than another; there are no bad temperaments. When you understand your own temperament, you can improve your career in these ways:

- by doing work that optimizes your natural strengths and preferences
- by communicating more effectively with others
- by relating to and understanding others better
- by identifying your weaknesses and blind spots

Not only does understanding your temperament help you professionally, but it is also invaluable in providing you insights about your family and friends. It gives you a framework with which to better understand natural differences and how those differences can result in conflict. You will be able to better communicate with your spouse and with other important people in your sphere of influence.

When I worked at El Paso Corporation, I brought in

Anne Murray, a consultant who specializes in helping people better understand themselves and others, to put on a day-long training session for all my field employees. Now, these are rough, tough, grizzled hourly employees who run from anything that sounds touchy-feely. But it only took a short time for Anne to win them over and for them to see the benefit of this training. The training was a huge hit, and it helped employees better understand themselves, their coworkers, and their bosses. At one of our plants in Mississippi, we had two long-service employees who didn't particularly like one another. They got along and spoke to each other when necessary, but that was about the extent of their relationship. During the lunch break, one of the employees went up to the other employee and shook his hand. He said to him, "I wasn't too excited about having to go through this training today. To be honest, I never liked you very much, but this morning I realized you are just a lot different than me. I hope we can be friends from now on." The relationship between these two coworkers radically improved once each of them better understand themselves as well as each other.

There are a number of excellent personality assessment tools on the market today. The Myers-Briggs Type Indicator (MBTI®) is the most widely used psychological instrument in the world, and it is based on Carl Jung's theory of the psyche. Jung's theories focus on how people gain information and make decisions. He believed that each person's psyche uses mental, or psychic, energy to process information. Some of the energy is conscious and some is unconscious. Jung identified eight processes used by the psyche that he believed that all people use. Through his studies, he identified differences in how people draw energy, acquire information, and evaluate information. He categorized these differences as opposite poles of three dimensions: energy, perception, and judgment.

Katherine Briggs, a contemporary of Carl Jung, learned of his work after she started making similar observations. As she studied his work, she became convinced that his theories had a practical application and that a person's personality type could be determined through a systematic process. But it was her daughter, Isabel Briggs Myers, who later developed the instrument now known as the MBTI® to determine a person's typological pattern. Based on her work and observations, she ended up adding a fourth dimension to Jung's that she called orientation. This dimension has to do with how people gather information and make decisions. The MBTI® now consists of the eight Jungian functions (which result in 16 possible personality types):

- Extroversion/Introversion
- Sensing/Intuition
- Thinking/Feeling
- Judging/Perceiving

The eight functions are also four separate dichotomies. People tend to prefer one alternative dichotomy over the polar opposite. It doesn't mean that the less-preferred alternative is never used. For example, people who are extroverts love being around and with other people, but there are times they may prefer being alone or may be more introverted. It's important to remember that:

- One psychological type isn't better than another.
- A psychological type is not a box into which we are put into by others, or into which we should put others.
- Type alone does not explain everything. (Within each of the sixteen types is an infinite variety of personalities, each different and valuable.)
- Type shouldn't be used for selecting your work, teammates, or life partner. (It looks at natural preferences, not abilities).
- All eight functions are used by each individual at least some of the time.

Understanding your unique personality type will not ensure that you find the perfect job for you, but knowing your natural personality type does enhance your understanding of your preferred occupational choices, interests, work environments, values, and development. For example, work environment tends to be more of a focus for an extrovert than for an introvert.

Another good instrument to take when considering job and career choices is the Strong Interest Inventory® Assessment. It assesses your interests among a broad range of occupations, work and leisure activities, and educational subjects. It is the most widely used career development instrument in the world and is a powerful tool for anyone considering changing careers, seeking a new career, or wanting more work–life balance.

There is more information about the MBTI® and other psychological instruments in the appendix. There you can also find out how to take the MBTI® to discover your unique type.

What are your unique personal values?

All of us have a set of values. We may not think about our values or even realize they are ours. They are usually determined by a number of external factors—our life experiences, our upbringing, our faith, and our education—that help shape and mold our core values or beliefs.

- **Values are something we hold dear, and they can be a person, material thing, quality, or activity.** Many of our values don't change over time. They become the cornerstones upon which we build our lives. People sometime confuse values with principles.

- **Principles are fundamental truths or guidelines for human conduct that have universal application.** Our values rarely change, but they can and sometimes do. Principles do not change.

People value different things. Some values can be viewed as positive by some people, but negatively by others. Some people value love, forgiveness, and kindness. Others value hatred, retribution, and violence. Terrorists share a set of common values that the vast majority of people in the world find unacceptable and repulsive. Why? Because terrorists see nothing wrong with killing innocent people, something that violates a principle shared by most people—that it is wrong to willfully, maliciously take another human life.

As I mentioned early, we have a set of core values. They become such an integral part of our lives that we seldom think about them. Values, whether good or bad, help drive our behaviors, and there are consequences associated with our behaviors. Take some time to carefully think about what or who you value. Make a list of these values now.

Your list may be short or long. For example, my list contains thirteen values. You can see my list in Appendix Two, which may help you as you think about and determine your own set of values. List your values below:

1.

2.

3.

4.

5.

Once you've developed your list of values, think about it and review it daily for several days. You might decide to add a value you left off the list or to delete a value you included at first. When you feel your list is complete, there's another step. For illustration purposes, let's say your list has eight values on it. Carefully think through your list of values: if you absolutely had to eliminate one value on the list, which one would it be? When you've eliminated that value, put a number 8 beside that value. Go through the same process of elimination the remaining seven values, ending up with only one value on your list—value 1. Eliminating the other values doesn't mean they aren't important to you, just that they are less important than some other values. Now get a sheet of paper and list your values from number *1* to *8*. This exercise forces you to prioritize your values, some more than others. I have found it to be very helpful to define what each value means. You and I may share the value of "family," but your definition of family may be significantly different from mine. Putting a definition to the value is adding meat to the bone, giving it substance and meaning.

When our life is in sync with our values, it takes on a new level of freedom. We don't let circumstances control us but are instead in control of our circumstances. By knowing our values, we begin to make time for important (though not necessarily urgent) activities and events. They become a compass to help guide us and keep us moving in the right direction. A few years ago, Karen Hughes was one of the most influential women in the American politics. She was a presidential advisor to George W. Bush, a position in which she daily brushed shoulders with some of the most powerful people in the world. She enjoyed her job and felt an enormous sense of loyalty to the President. Karen valued both her family and her career, but she began to realize that her family was a higher priority value than her career. Upon realizing this, she decided to quit her Washington job and move her family back to Texas, a place she thought better for raising a family. She was willing to give up daily contact with the President, the most powerful person in the world, as well as having significant influence on administration policies and decisions, to spend more time with her family. I admire Karen for making a tough decision that was something she needed to do—and, more importantly, did—because she understood her personal values.

You and I will most likely not have to make the same choice Karen did, but knowing our values helps us make the right personal choices each day. One day my son Josh stopped by the house and wanted me to help him work on his car. It was a busy day for me, and I really didn't have the time to help him. But as I thought about my values, I realized that spending time with my son was of greater value to me than my career was, so I dropped what I was doing to help him. Knowing our values and living according to them helps us keep our lives and activities in the right perspective.

Purpose: Putting it All Together

We began this chapter talking about discovering your life purpose—your reason for being. Your purpose statement should answer the question, "Why do I exist?" A wise friend told me one time, "It's more important to be than to do." It's easy for us to let the doing part of our lives overshadow the being part of our lives. Doing comes easily for most of us. But are we doing the right things, the important things, with our lives? Once we discover our purpose, we start aligning the things we do with our reason for being, and life takes on real meaning. I'm convinced that people want to live a life of purpose. They yearn for a life that has meaning and fulfillment. It's no accident that Rick Warren's *The Purpose Driven® Life* is the best-selling book in American history, with over twenty-five million copies sold.

I hope you've taken the time while exploring this chapter to look at all the things in your life that make you unique—your passion, personality, abilities, education, experiences, skills, and values. All these things have helped shape and mold you into the person you are today, but more importantly the person you can be. Review your lists, think about the things you wrote down, and write your own purpose statement below. This is the same process I used several years ago when developing my life purpose statements of the things I am designed to do:

- Know God in a personal way
- Grow to my God-given potential and help others to do the same
- Sow seeds in the lives of others
- Show love to my family and friends
- Go through life without excuses and regrets—with passion and purpose

Don't get hung up on trying to make your purpose statement absolutely perfect. Begin by getting your thoughts down on paper; you can modify and tweak them later. It's time to write your own statement by completing the following sentence.

My life's purpose is to _____

_____

_____

_____.

CHAPTER SEVEN

Keeping Your Eye on the Target

I know the price of success: dedication, hard work, and the unremitting devotion to the thing you want to see happen.

FRANK LLOYD WRIGHT

A s I write this chapter, it's the day after Super Bowl XLII. Last night, the New England Patriots played the New York Giants to determine who would be world champions. The Patriots were also trying to complete a perfect season and become the first team in professional football to go undefeated the entire season, winning nineteen games. The Miami Dolphins are the only team to have gone undefeated in what was at the time a 17-game season.

Do you think the Patriots and Giants showed up for the big game without any game plan or goal other than having fun? Can you imagine Brady or Manning going into the huddle and saying, "Guys, just line up; when I say hut, I'm sure you'll figure out what to do?" Neither the Patriots nor the Giants got to football's ultimate game by showing up at practice each day, and at the games each weekend, just to go through the motions. Instead, both of them had a definite game plan that complimented their team's strengths and exploited their opponent's weaknesses. The game plan was meticulously thought out, and they knew exactly what plays they would run in each game situation. Hours and hours of practice, film study, and game planning had taken place with one goal in mind: winning the Super Bowl. Before the season even started, every player knew what the team goals were for the season—win their division, win their conference, and win the Super Bowl. Great football teams and world championships don't just happen.

Great lives don't just happen either. Yet many people go through the game of life without having a plan or goals. They go through the motions day after day, wondering why nothing positive happens. They keep doing the same things over and over and then wonder why they keeping getting the same results. Your most immediate goal is to find another job. How quickly you need to find the job largely depends on your financial situation. If you didn't receive much severance and don't have a lot of savings to tide you over, your time frame for finding another job is shortened. If this is this case for you, financial reality requires that you find a job quickly. Many people find themselves in this situation, because many companies can't or don't pay much severance, or employees weren't at a company long enough to get a larger severance payout. This situation is more the rule than the exception today. The U.S. Department of Labor reports that one in four workers has been employed by his or her present employer for less than a year—and that one in two workers has been at his or her place of employment less than five years. If you find yourself in this situation, no one will fault you for quickly finding another job, even if it's not the ideal job for you. If you do this, I encourage you not to be satisfied long-term with the job you took unless it really is the ideal job for you. Instead, you should view this as a temporary job stop while you go through the process I've been talking about. As you continue to seek your ideal job, you can make the job change on your own terms instead of on someone else's. It is easier to find another job when you're employed than when you're unemployed. Unfortunately, many people who take the first job offered or a job for which they are overqualified end up staying there until they can't stand it anymore or until they are fired. It's easy to get trapped in a comfort zone, settling for second best rather than continue to pursue the right job for you. But don't let it happen to you. If you don't control your destiny, someone will control if for you. It's your choice.

If you were fortunate enough to get a good severance package or have enough savings in the bank, you can afford to take more time to find another job. Block out time on your calendar to go through the process we've discussed in this book. When you do so, you're investing time and energy in yourself and taking proactive steps to shape your destiny and future.

Developing Your Game Plan

Just as the Giants and Patriots entered the Super Bowl with a well-thought-out, carefully crafted game plan, you, too, need to develop your own career game plan. Your plan should be written down where you can review it daily. Many people resist writing their plans down or don't see any value in doing so, saying that their plans are in their heads. So are hundreds of other plans and ideas that seldom come to fruition. Plans may be floating around in your mind, but you will not remember them and focus on them unless you write them down. Something powerful happens when you write down your goals and plans.

If you study the lives of successful people, you will find that they have the habit of writing down their plans and goals. They know exactly where they want to go in life, and they have a plan to get them there. It's their road map

> *The weakest ink is stronger than the strongest mind.*

or blueprint to success. We will discuss goal-setting later. Here are five reasons why you should commit your plan to paper:

1. A written plan helps you crystallize your thinking. Putting your plan on paper helps you to clarify your thinking. As you read your plan, you can tweak and refine it to reflect your latest thinking. Keeping your plan in your head makes it too easy to forget key parts and to make both strategic and tactical mistakes. When I started flying, I quickly learned the importance of having a preflight checklist and flight plan. Every pilot goes through a written checklist before taking off, even those who have flown a thousand times before. Why? Failure to properly check an item on the list could have catastrophic consequences, killing the pilot and passengers. Thankfully, failure to have a written plan will not get you killed, but it may cause you to wander around for years, accomplishing little or nothing at all.

2. A written plan provides self-accountability. When we have written plans and review them, we consciously begin to hold ourselves accountable for completing them. It makes it harder for us to ignore or forget about what we need to be doing.

3. A written plan keeps you focused. A well-written, job/career plan focuses on the mission-critical steps we need to be taking to find another job. You know exactly what needs to be accomplished, and by what specific date. You even begin to see your next steps in your mind's eye. The ability to focus on what needs to be done, and then to do it, is what separates successful people from unsuccessful people. Successful people don't get distracted from their plans. They stay on course until their plans are completed. Have you ever thought about buying a particular brand and model of automobile? If so, you probably noticed as you drove around town or on the interstate a large number of automobiles just like the brand and model you were considering. You begin to see them everywhere. Were they not there before? Of course they were—but you weren't focused on them then. Let me demonstrate to you the power of focus. For the next few minutes, I want you to think about anything *but* the color red. Wherever you are, look around but don't think about or notice anything that's red. Forget about red cars, red roses, and red dresses. Stop and take a couple of minutes to try this simple exercise.

How did you do? I suspect you had trouble focusing on anything but red. Everywhere you looked you were immediately drawn to anything red. It validates the simple but powerful concept of *focus*.

4. A written plan builds self-confidence. As you take action, completing the steps of your plan, you gain self-confidence, moving closer and closer to the accomplishment of your plan. Small successes breed larger ones. It feels good to check off of your list a part of your plan that you've completed.

5. A written plan moves you toward your final goal. A good plan always has an ultimate objective, and each step you take in the plan moves you closer to it. Soon your plan begins to work like the force of a magnet, pulling you closer and closer to your objective. As you go about your daily activities, your mind will be working subconsciously to move you toward your objective.

I trust you see the benefits of developing a written plan for how to go about finding your new job or career. A good plan needs to be **specific**, **actionable**, **behavioral**, and **measurable.**

But your plan doesn't need to be complicated—keep it

simple! I've seen companies develop elaborate, detailed plans that would take hours to read. They look great, sound impressive, and are full of charts, graphs, and numbers. They become known as SPOTS, or Strategic Plans On Top Shelf. These plans end up being shelf art and are never looked at again until it's time to prepare next year's plan. You aren't developing a strategic plan, but you do need to plan how to successfully find your new job. If you develop a written plan, you will be ahead of 90 percent of the other people looking for a job. Many people don't develop plans because they think it's too difficult or because they don't know how to go about developing one; but a one-page plan is all you need.

- **Specific:** A good plan is very specific. It doesn't talk about generalities but is specific about desired outcomes, behaviors, and "next steps." General, vague plans don't provide the focus or create the energy needed to compel people to execute plans.
- **Actionable:** A plan needs to identify what actions or steps must be taken to achieve the objective. By developing your list of subsequent steps, you recognize exactly what needs to be done and in what order. As you execute each step, you move closer to your objective. You should constantly be asking yourself, "What is the next step?"
- **Behavioral:** Many people forget this step when developing plans, but it's critical to the success of the plan. There are certain behaviors you must do daily, weekly, and at other intervals as you look for your new job.

These are the things that need to fill your calendar each day. To be a great musician, athlete, artist, or business-person, you must master the basics and do certain things each day to improve your skills. The key is being disciplined to practice these behaviors daily, even on the days you don't feel like doing them.

• **Measurable**: There is an old adage in business: what gets measured gets done. I've found this to be absolutely true in people's professional and personal lives. Measures are milestones to help you monitor your progress on your job journey and to let you know when you succeeded in meeting your objective. Measurement lets you know at any moment exactly where you stand.

It's important that your plan incorporate all these components. Let's get started. The plan has three simple, but highly effective steps:

Step 1: Objective. The objective is your desired end result. As Stephen Covey teaches, let's begin with the end in mind. Thinking about and carefully defining our desired outcome increases our chance of achieving it. Be sure to make your objective specific. For example, "finding another job" is not specific. Let's say you're an accountant—your objective might read, "Obtain a senior level accountant position with a mid-sized accounting firm making $80,000 annually in Hometown, America, by June 1, 2008." An objective like this is much more effective than is a passive objective of "getting another accounting job" (Harkavy 2007). Be as specific as you can when writing your objective.

Step 2: Behaviors. Behaviors are daily or weekly actions you will do to move you toward your desired objective. You will need to be disciplined, focusing yourself on making sure that you do these behaviors at the times you have them scheduled. If you find you are having trouble doing these, find someone—a friend, a family member, or someone else—to hold you accountable to master these behaviors as scheduled. When you finish writing down your plan, give a copy to your accountability partner and ask him or her to meet with you weekly so that you can report to your partner how well you're doing on each part of your plan. This is one of the inherent benefits for those people who use outplacement firms, which have coaches and counselors who work with their clients to ensure that they are working according to plans. Sometimes we need someone to help hold us accountable. If you struggle with doing your required behaviors, I strongly encourage you to get an accountability partner and to insist that, each week, or whenever you meet or talk, this person ask you tough questions about how you're doing.

> *"Winners develop a habit of doing the things losers don't like to do."*

There are several important behaviors you might want

to master as part of your job search plan. Here are some examples:

- Call or follow up on five people on your networking list.
- Review the job ads in your local newspaper each week, checking into every job that fits your objective.
- Practice your answers to several potential interview questions each day.
- Send handwritten thank-you notes daily to anyone you interviewed with or networked with the previous day.
- Exercise thirty minutes each day to keep you feeling strong and fit as well as to sweat away a few extra pounds.
- Spend ten minutes daily reading something motivational or uplifting.
- Conduct a "post mortem" on job interviews to evaluate what you did well and what you need to improve.
- Meet with your accountability partner weekly to review how well you're doing at implementing each of your stated behaviors and at executing your next steps.
- Attend a meeting each week or month that will increase your networking opportunities.

Whatever behaviors you decide need to be part of your daily, weekly, or even monthly routine should be scheduled on your calendar each day. Again, don't make the fatal mistake of not writing them down on your calendar. Keep doing your scheduled actions even when you don't want to and don't feel like it. Make them a habit. I've had a plaque in my office for years that reads: "Winners develop a habit of doing the things losers don't like to do."

Step 3: Next steps. These are a list of the mission-critical steps you need to take to find another job. "Mission-critical" refers to those three to five steps or projects that are truly necessary for you to find a job within whatever time frame you established for finding your new job. Each step should be listed in chronological order and should be scheduled on your calendar. If one of the steps is actually a project with substeps, it helps to identify the substeps, writing them down also, along with their deadlines for completion.

A few years ago I read about a concept called "mind mapping." Mind mapping uses a diagram to represent words, ideas, concepts, plans, or other things that are linked to and arranged around a central key word or idea. Supporting words, ideas, and concepts radiate from the center, and are linked by a linc or arrow. Because I am a visual learner, this approach has helped me better understand and remember the information I'm mapping. It may help you if you're also a visual learner. On the next page is an example of a job search plan mapped using the mind mapping technique. At the center of the map is a job objective stated actively. The surrounding connected boxes are behaviors that must be mastered and executed routinely. The next steps of major milestones to be accomplished are listed at the bottom of the plan, as is the target date for each action or project.

Next Steps

December 1
1. Finalize and print 50 résumés
2. Begin an exercising program to achieve my ideal weight of 180

December 15
3. Create and organize my networking list

January 10
4. Call everyone on my networking list

January 20
5. Select and meet with my accountability partner to establish my schedule

January 22
6. Develop my list of networking opportunities

June 1
7. Begin my new job

Daily Behaviors

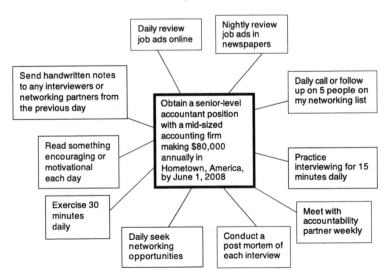

Putting your plan to work

I hope you've now discovered that a plan can be simple and effective. It doesn't have to be complicated or lengthy. I used just this planning approach when I lost my job, and I eventually decided to start my own consulting company. After starting my company, I continued to use this same format for developing the business plan for each component of my consulting practice—consulting, coaching, speaking, and writing. My business plan has four simple but powerful pages that drive my behaviors, directing me one step at a time toward my stated outcomes.

Once you develop a plan, how do you best use it? Your plan is a road map, and its purpose is to guide you to your final outcome (destination)—finding a new job. But your plan must be flexible; you may need to add or revise next steps or modify behaviors as you move toward your outcome. Here are suggestions on how to get the most out of your plan.

• **Review your plan daily.** Your plan will not help you if you don't know what it says. Find time each day to review the plan, whether the first thing each morning or before you go to bed each night. Continually reviewing your plan will help propel you toward your outcome as it becomes imprinted in your memory.

* **Use your plan to drive your priorities.** Any plan is worthless unless it is executed. Never forget that the secret to your future is hidden in your daily agenda. The decisions you made yesterday and your actions today will determine your future. Schedule time for each behavior in your plan. If exercising thirty minutes daily is part of your plan, schedule it in your calendar each day, and do it. Perhaps the best time for you to check job advertisements is each evening after dinner. If so, make it a priority, and schedule it in your calendar. It's best to schedule each behavior at a consistent time daily or weekly so that it becomes a habit. Experts say that it takes thirty consecutive days for a behavior to become a habit.

* **Use your plan for your accountability meetings.** Share your job search plan with your accountability partner. He or she can then ask you how you're doing with each behavior and "next step" action. Your partner may even suggest adding some additional behaviors or milestones that you haven't thought about.

* **Revise your plan as necessary.** Your behaviors shouldn't change much, if any, throughout your job search. The next step actions and milestones will most likely need to be adjusted or added to as you implement your plan.

• **Use your plan to help you stay focused.** Staying focused and keeping your eye on your outcome is critical. Your plan will assist you in doing this, particularly as you master the necessary behaviors you'll put on your plan. Don't get distracted or discouraged along the way. You will find a job as long as you continually take positive steps each day toward your goal. You may not see or sense your progress at times, but each step you take and each behavior you master will move you closer to your desired outcome.

Managing Yourself

You've developed a sound job search plan, and every day you're scheduling on your calendar the behaviors you are going to master during your search. It is important to keep your calendar with you at all times. Referring to it during the course of each day will help you stay focused and on track. In addition to using your calendar to take control of your mission-critical behaviors, you should use it to schedule time to prioritize the personal values you listed in Chapter Six. For example, if one of your values is family, be sure to schedule time to do things with your family. By making time for the things you value, your life will suddenly become more meaningful and fulfilling. Your calendar is a tool to help you manage the events of your life. Your time—all 86,400 seconds of each day—will always get filled up and used up by someone or something. It's your responsibility to make sure that you are controlling the events of your life—that they aren't controlling you.

I once saw a demonstration by a time management expert that made a lasting impression on me. He placed a wide-mouthed gallon jar on the table in front of him. Next to the jar was a collection of fist-sized rocks. He carefully filled the jar with the big rocks until he could fit no more.

He asked the group watching is demonstration, "Is the jar full?"

Everyone responded, "Yes."

He then pulled a large bowl of gravel from under the table and poured the gravel into the jar. The gravel fit into the spaces between the rocks, and he again asked, "Is the jar full?"

"Probably not," was now the group's reply.

He reached for another bowl, this one filled with sand. He dumped the sand into the jar. The sand filled the spaces not occupied by rocks or gravel. Once more, he asked, "Is the jar full?"

"No," everyone answered.

Finally, he reached for a pitcher of water and poured water into the jar until it was filled to the top. The time management expert looked at the group and asked, "What is the point of my illustration?"

One person replied, "That no matter how full your schedule is, you can always fit one more thing into it."

"No!" the expert responded.

The point of this illustration is, "If you don't put the big rocks in first, you'll never get all the things in the jar!"

Too many people fill their time jars, or lives, with sand and pebbles. It quickly becomes full, and the big rocks can't go into the jar at all. The big rocks are your values—the things that are most important to you. Schedule them first, and you will be amazed at how you will be able to fit all the other less important events in your life around them. As you search for your new job, the behaviors and next steps are big rocks, too.

I don't know what time management system works best for you. During my career I've tried so many different systems that I have lost count. I've tried electronic calendars and paper-based calendar systems. Each one has it own advantages. Today, I keep my calendar on my BlackBerry® phone, which synchronizes with the Microsoft® Outlook calendar on my computer. I don't know what type of system you use, but if you don't have one, I strongly encourage you to develop one you can use during your job search.

I think that, as with your plan, a simple time-management system works the best. It should be one you can easily carry with you and quickly refer to. If someone calls you on your cell phone and wants to schedule an interview with you two weeks down the road, you don't want to tell them you will have to call them back after you've had a chance to look at your calendar. When I was hiring someone, it always bothered me if the person had to call me back to confirm the interview or meeting. The impression I got was that such an interviewee wasn't well organized. In my mind, the person had a strike against him before he had even interviewed for the job. Your calendar is a powerful tool; always make sure you have yours with you at all times.

Consider Keeping a Journal

I've been journaling for the last two decades. It's a habit that has served me well over the years. A journal is a great tool to record your thoughts, ideas, conversations, commitments, plans, and to-do lists. I find it very helpful to have one book in which I can record things quickly as I think of an idea or commit myself to do things. One of my personal values is organization, and my journal helps me stay organized and in control.

I've been surprised at the number of people who also

journal, including President Reagan and billionaire entre-
preneur Richard Branson. Here is an excerpt from a 2004
Fortune article about Branson:

> Branson is hilariously low tech. He never uses a com-
> puter. He uses his black book and writes all his ideas down
> in longhand, including the e-mails he will dictate to his
> secretary. Immediate things to remember—like phone
> messages—he writes on the back of his hand. Indeed, a
> glance at Branson's black book shows that after three
> full decades, he is still as energetic, peripatetic, and fully
> engaged as ever. The current diary (he began keeping them
> when he was sixteen) begins in March, and it includes every
> brainstorm, every business conversation, every meaningful
> valuation of any business deal, any substantive conversa-
> tion he has had with his advisors, his investment bankers,
> his partners. It includes musings about a possible new cel-
> lular company in Canada, a low-cost airline in Japan, and
> another transatlantic balloon race. He has filled page after
> page with his exhaustive efforts to get his hands on the
> Concorde—details of talks with Airbus executives, former
> Concorde pilots, and engineers—and he is clearly irked
> that he won't succeed. But the book also includes the fol-
> lowing: "Michael Jackson wanted to come [to Necker] next
> week." And several days later: "Nicole Kidman said she'd
> love to play tennis." It includes a letter he has penned to

Nelson Mandela, urging him to do something about the war in Iraq. There is a quote from his wife Joan: "Extremism in the pursuit of excellence is not a vice." Woven in are amusing stories . . . Why did the British immigration lady check his passport, when it was so obvious she knew who he was? "We wanted to know your age," she tells him. His daughter Holly has been to Prince William's twenty-first birthday party, where there was an enormous elephant made of ice, with straight vodka pouring from its trunk. As Holly leaned forward, mouth open, to taste the vodka, she caught a glimpse of the Queen, surveying the scene with a disparaging look on her face (Morris 2003).

If Branson can run his vast empire from a black composition book, you can employ the same tactic to help you find a job.

As you start your job search, journaling is a great behavior to include as a daily behavior you will master in the plan you developed earlier. During your search, you will be talking to many different people, and a journal is a good place to record your conversations along with any follow-up actions. You can keep your network list in your journal. Like your calendar, keep your journal with you at all times so that when you think of new names to add to your list you can do it then, or so that when someone calls you, you can note key points from the conversation. I also found that putting my thoughts, feelings, frustrations, and victories down on paper was therapeutic for me during my career transition. Recording the progress I made each day during my career change gave me confidence as I progressed toward my targeted outcome: starting my own business.

In keeping with our theme of "simpler is better," a journal can be anything from a spiral notebook to a leather-bound journal—whatever works best for you. I personally use a 8½ by 11-inch, spiral-bound hardcover notebook made by Cambridge. It has a couple of pocket inserts inside the front cover for storing loose sheets of paper, travel itineraries, and other information I need to keep. I like the letter-size journal because it is easy to slip loose pages inside the journal. I strongly suggest that you print out your job search plan and put it in your journal so that you can review it daily. If you use Outlook for your calendar and it isn't synced to your phone or PDA, you can print the monthly calendar pages and carry those in your journal to ensure that you are managing your time wisely. It's a great behavior to learn, and as it becomes a habit you will find that it will also serve you well in your new job or career.

CHAPTER EIGHT

Marketing Yourself

"The way to get started is to quit talking and begin doing."

WALT DISNEY

Your new job is to find a job. This is a positive mindset to take on as you start your job search. Treat looking for a job like having a job. When you were employed, you worked specific hours each week and had a regular routine. As you look for a job, commit yourself to setting aside a certain number of hours each day to work on your search plan. Develop a job search routine for each day, schedule it in your calendar, and discipline yourself to follow through on your scheduled actions.

Many people find it easy to get distracted when looking

for a job. After all, there is no office or workplace to go to each day, and hanging around the house each day offers too many tempting distractions—like watching television or taking a nap. One of the advantages offered by outplacement firms is that they provide a work space for their clients to use each day during their job search. Unfortunately, outplacement facilities are usually provided only to more senior-level employees. Most employees conduct their job searches from home. If you're conducting your job search from home, it's critical that you use a disciplined approach. If you don't have an office or study at home, find some place to serve as your new job search office, such as the dining room or a spare bedroom. Most formal dining rooms aren't used very often, and the table makes for a good desk area. Once you've found a place to work from, it's time to go to work. The search plan you developed earlier will most likely include four standard but critical job search steps: developing a correct mindset, creating your résumé, using your networking, and honing your interviewing skills.

Developing a Good Mindset

As you're in the process of looking for a new job, it's important to maintain the right mindset. You may not have looked for another job since getting your first one, or you may now be looking for a different type of job. The attitude you adopt as you begin your job search journey will go a long way toward helping you find another job. Here are five things you should make part of your mindset:

1. Your new job. Your new full-time job is simple: to find another job. View the search process as a job you work at every day until you find another job—one that will pay you. Stay with the plan you developed earlier and keep working at it one step at a time. Keep asking yourself, "What is my next step?" Once you decide on your next step, take it immediately. Don't procrastinate—do it now. No one is going to do it for you. It's your job to do it, so be relentless in the pursuit of another job.

2. Stay positive. Decide to stay positive no matter what comes your way. Every time a negative thought enters your mind, displace it with a positive thought. If an interview doesn't work out, don't let it get you down. The greatest hitters in baseball strike out almost twice as often as they get hits. But they keep swinging, knowing that it's only a matter of time before they get on base. Some people find it helpful to develop some positive affirmations to read at least daily. This is a good way to keep you focused on the positive. Be sure to write your affirmations down on paper, and discipline yourself to read them at least once daily.

3. Stick-to-it-ivity. Realize that you will have some not-so-good days in your job search. When you do, don't give up and start feeling defeated or sorry for yourself. When you get knocked down, get back up and keep going, always pressing forward toward your outcome.

4. Be realistic. It will be great if the first offer to come along is exactly what you're looking for in a new job or career, but chances are it won't be, so accept reality for what it is and learn to deal with it. It may take you weeks or months to find another job, but you will find one in due time. Some people cultivate unrealistic expectations and are crushed when they don't achieve them. Expecting to find a new job in a week isn't a realistic expectation for most people. You can be positive and realistic at the same time.

5. Celebrate victories. We tend to focus on our failures more than on our successes. We think about all the things we didn't get done and forget about all the things we did accomplish. Sometimes, when my former management team was grousing about all the things we still needed to accomplish as a team, I would stop them and take a time-out. We would go through the process of listing on a board everything we had accomplished in a certain time period—month, quarter, or year—and everyone was invariably shocked at how much the team had accomplished. They went from feeling bad about themselves to feeling like winners. Each evening in your journal or notebook, write down everything you accomplished that particular day in your search, no matter how small it may seem at the time. It will help energize and encourage you to continue making progress the next day. Don't forget, each step takes you closer and closer to your desired outcome. You may not be able to see the outcome except in your mind's eye, but you know you are continually narrowing the gap with each step. Take time to recognize and celebrate your victories, whether small or large.

Creating Your Résumé

In your past job, you may have been in operations, finance, administration, engineering, or some other functional area. It really doesn't matter. As you look for a new job, realize that you just got promoted. Congratulations! You're now vice president of marketing, and the product you're about to market is . . . yourself! Like any great marketer, you know your product's strengths, capabilities, uniqueness, and advantages over competing products. To sell your product, you simply have to find someone who has a need for it and then convince them that you're the best person to fill that need.

Earlier, you developed your job plan. It should have included some next steps, one of which should have been developing your résumé. Your résumé is an important element in your marketing campaign. It will not land you a job by itself, but it's a calling card that will open—or close—potential job doors for you. Your résumé is your career story and lets a potential buyer know what you've done in the past, which is the best indicator of what you can do in the future for another company. Putting together a good résumé isn't as hard as you might think when you follow some simple, proven guidelines. Let's take a look at what résumés are:

Types of résumés

There are basically two types of résumé—chronological and functional.

1. Chronological. This is the most common type of résumé used today, and most hiring authorities are used to seeing its familiar structure. It is easier to read and understand, because it flows chronologically. This type of résumé works best for those who have several years of continuous work history and job titles that will be meaningful toward a new career objective.

Your résumé should list your job history in reverse order

from your current or most recent job to your first. This is true when listing your education also. Don't waste valuable space describing jobs you held more than ten years ago. Employers will focus on your most recent job accomplishments. Make sure that for any jobs you've had in the last ten years you list your accomplishments, describing your last job in the most detail.

2. Functional. The functional résumé works best for those who need to emphasize skills or abilities more than dates, who have gaps in their job histories, or whose work histories and job titles don't match their desired job very well. Instead of listing job titles and dates, the résumé is structured around functional headings that describe areas of expertise. For example, some typical headings might describe leadership, planning, organizing, problem solving, computer skills, and so forth.

Regardless of which type of résumé you use, you should do certain basic things to create a résumé that stands out:

Résumé pointers

1. Think outcomes again. The desired outcome of your résumé is to effectively sell yourself and to create interest in the eyes of the buyer. Every hiring person is looking for someone who is going to solve a problem for them. When developing your résumé, put yourself in the seat of the hiring authority and ask yourself, "Does this résumé look like someone who can help our company be successful?" If the answer isn't yes, you need to rethink your résumé.

2. Pique their interest. The résumé is your calling card and must create interest on the part of the hiring authority. You want someone to look at your résumé and decide one thing: this looks like someone we should bring in for an interview.

3. Keep it less than two pages. Many HR professionals recommend that a résumé be only one page long. Others will tell you that if you have more than ten years of experience, you will need at least two pages. So don't feel as though you have to limit yourself to one page, but remember that anything more than a two-page résumé is too long and probably won't be read—or will be viewed negatively.

4. Be positive. Don't include negative points or points a company will not find relevant.

5. Use bullets. Bulleted items don't require complete sentences, thus taking up less space—and they stand out. Don't bullet everything, but do use bullets consistently throughout your résumé to list key items, such as your accomplishments.

6. Focus on accomplishments. Too many résumés list

activities performed in each job. If you're trying to get a job as a marketing manager, the hiring authority will probably be the director of marketing, who will know perfectly well the duties of a marketing representative, senior marketing representative, or account executive. Although it is customary to provide a sentence describing the position's responsibilities (activities) next to your job title, immediately below that you should list bulleted items of your accomplishments: how you added value to the organization.

Which of the following descriptions is more impressive on a résumé?

Marketing Manager

Oversaw a staff of ten marketing representatives responsible for Florida, Georgia, and South Carolina for a large chemical company. Prepared annual marketing plan, hired and trained staff members, conducted weekly staff meeting, and hosted annual customer meeting.

Marketing Manager: Florida, Georgia, South Carolina

Managed a team of ten marketers for ABC Chemical company, including developing and executing our strategic marketing plan, hiring and developing staff, and improving customer relations.

- Grew sales by 22 percent ($1.2 million) yearly
- Increased customer satisfaction by 35 percent
- Reduced staff turnover by 28 percent
- Lowered warehousing costs by 31 percent in two years

Clearly, the last résumé looks more impressive because it highlights accomplishments, showing how the person added value to the organization.

7. Use numbers, dollars, and percentages. These types of symbols are quantifiable and measurable and look impressive on your résumé. They show what you accomplished and indicate that you are results-oriented.

8. Education. Your education and academic training should come after your job history. If you're college-educated, don't include your high school on your résumé. If you're not college educated, you will want to include your high school on your résumé. Only list your GPA if it was higher than 3.0 on a 4.0 scale or if you graduated with honors. If it has been years since you graduated from college or technical school, few employers will be interested in your GPA.

9. Use action words. Action words create a sense of energy and accomplishment. They paint a mental portrait of a doer—of someone who gets things done and makes things happen. Here are some examples of action words:

Active nouns and modifiers—*ability, actively, adaptive, competent, competitive, effectiveness, proficient, qualified, technical.*

Active verbs—*accelerated, accomplished, achieved, administered, aligned, approved, conducted, completed, controlled, coordinated, created, delegated, designed, developed, directed, established, evaluated, expanded, expedited, finished, finalized, generated, increased, influenced, implemented, improved, instructed, led, leveraged, maintained, managed, marketed, motivated, modified, operated, organized, performed, planned, produced, programmed, proposed, qualified, quantified, recommended, reconciled, reviewed, reorganized, revised, restructured, scheduled, simplified, streamlined, solved, supervised, supported, trained, taught, used, wrote.*

10. Contact Information. Make sure to include your contact information on your résumé, including your mailing address, telephone number, and e-mail address (be sure to include your contact information on the second page as well). I can't tell you the number of employers and headhunters who see résumés that omit this information and can't figure out how to get in touch with their authors.

11. Personal Information. Limit your personal information to your contact information only. Do not include irrelevant information such as age, date of birth, marital status, or number, gender, or age of children.

12. Job gaps. HR professionals, headhunters, and managers are trained to look for time gaps in résumés. Gaps immediately throw up a red flag. Be honest about gaps and don't hide them. However, it's not necessary when showing several years of work history to include months. For example, it is acceptable to list your job history by years:

Zco Plastics: Bowling Green, KY

Plant Manager   1999–2006

13. Listing job references. Most experts suggest that you not include references on your résumé. Instead, have a separate piece of paper available with your references listed on it. You should have at least three references who know you and your capabilities well. Make sure to get permission from the references to use them, and always call them to let them know to whom you gave your list of references and for what job you're applying. Should your references get a phone call, they won't be surprised by it—and, hopefully, you coached them to provide feedback and comments supporting the job you're being considered for. A lot of people forget to contact and coach their references; failing to do so can hurt their chances of getting a job.

14. Salary information. It's best not to include your salary history on your résumé. If it's too high, it might automatically exclude you from some jobs, and if it's too low the hiring person may feel that you're underqualified. You will be asked to provide your salary information when you complete the company's employment application, a time when you will be in a better position from which to negotiate your salary.

15. Use an appropriate font and size. The most commonly used font is Times New Roman, but you can use other common fonts, such as Arial. Avoid distinctive, artsy fonts unless you're applying for a highly creative or artistic position. You should use a font size of 12 points, and in no case smaller than 10 points.

16. Have someone proof your résumé. Have a friend or family member carefully proof your résumé for content and errors. Typos in a résumé are unacceptable and show a lack of attention to detail. Better yet, find a human resources professional or headhunter and ask whether they will critique your résumé for you. They can offer you unbiased and invaluable feedback and might even give you a lead for your job search.

17. Printing your résumé. Your résumé is a reflection of you. Your résumé must look professional to help it stand out from the other (sometimes hundreds) of résumés competing for hiring authorities' attentions. Keep the following in mind when printing your résumé:

a. If you're mailing your résumé, use high-quality résumé paper made of 24–40 lb. cotton. You can use colored paper, but stick to white, ivory, or gray. Résumé paper can be bought at any office supply store and adds a touch of elegance that hiring authorities can both see and feel. Use matching paper for your cover letter and envelope (9 by 12 inches).

b. Use a high-quality laser printer.

c. Don't fold your résumé.

d. Don't put samples in your résumé.

e. Never use Wite-out or handwrite changes on your résumé or any correspondence. Simply reprint a corrected version.

It should go without saying, but make sure the information on your résumé is accurate and truthful. Many people have lost jobs after being hired when it was discovered that they falsified information on their résumés. Most employers will validate key information on your résumé or job application. Honesty always pays off, although I certainly don't recommend the slightly-too-honest approach of the seventy-five-year-old senior citizen who applied for a job with Wal-Mart and filled out this job application:

Sex: Not lately, but I am looking for the right woman (or at least one who will cooperate).

Desires Position: President or Vice President. But seriously, whatever's available. If I was in a position to be picky, I wouldn't be applying here in the first place.

Desired Salary: $185,000 a year plus stock options and a Michael Ovitz–style severance package. If that's not possible, make an offer and we can haggle.

Education: Yes.

Last Position Held: Target for middle management hostility.

Previous Salary: A lot less than I'm worth.

Most Notable Achievement: My incredible collection of stolen pens and post-it notes.

Reason for Leaving: It sucked.

Hours Available to Work: Any.

Preferred Hours: 1:30–3:30 PM Monday, Tuesday, and Thursday.

Do You Have Any Special Skills? Yes, but they're better suited to a more intimate environment.

May We Contact Your Current Employer? If I had one, would I be here?

Do You Have a Car? I think the more appropriate question here would be, "Do you have a car that runs?"

What Would You Like to Be Doing in Five Years?
Living in the Bahamas with a fabulously wealthy, dumb, sexy, blonde supermodel who thinks I'm the greatest thing since sliced bread. Actually, I'd like to be doing that now.

Nearest Relative: Seven miles.

By the way, Wal-Mart hired him—they loved his sense of humor.

The Art of Interviewing

A professionally prepared résumé will help get you in the door for an interview. Your résumé focuses on your past, and the interview focuses on your future. But, because one of the best indicators of your future performance is your past performance, your interviewer will spend considerable time asking you about your past. It's very important that you be prepared to answer questions about anything on your résumé, so come to the interview prepared and ready to sell yourself, because that's what you'll be doing during the interview.

Some people aren't comfortable talking about themselves—which is understandable. But in any interview you are the only one able to talk about you, so it's up to you to sell yourself. The interviewer is expecting you to do this—and the other people you're competing with for the job are selling themselves. As a friend once told me, "Go ahead and toot your own horn—after all, you know the tune better than anyone else!" He's absolutely correct. Go ahead and blow your own horn: just be careful you don't blow it too loud or too long.

Interviews are the most common way of selecting candidates for a job. Unfortunately, interviews aren't always good predictors of future success, because some people don't interview as well as others. You can be the best candidate in the world for a job and be beaten out by someone less qualified who happens to interview extremely well. Also, interviewers bring their own biases—both conscious and subconscious—into the interview process. Here are some common biases you should be aware of:

The mirror effect: People like to hire people who are like themselves. They tend to select people with whom they share personal characteristics or interests.

First impressions: The old cliché is often true—you only get one chance to make a good first impression. First impressions can be hard to overcome, particularly for interviewers who haven't been trained to be aware of this tendency. The interviewer may rush to a snap decision based on something a candidate says or does early during the interview.

Stereotyping: Stereotyping occurs when an interviewer holds generalized opinions about how people of a certain race, religion, gender, national origin, creed, or even career choice think, act, or feel. For example, some interviewers may think that accountants are supposed to be quiet and reserved, but that isn't always the case.

> *In business or in football, it takes a lot of unspectacular preparation to produce spectacular results.*
>
> ROGER STAUBACH, HALL OF FAME FOOTBALL PLAYER

Nonverbal: The interviewer may draw conclusions about candidates based on the way they talk, dress, or look.

Halo effect: This can occur when an interviewer allows something he or she values or thinks is extremely important to overshadow other information and facts about candidates.

Poor questioning techniques: Good interviewers will ask a set of predetermined questions to all candidates so that each candidate's answers can be compared against those of the other. Many interviewers don't use this approach, however, and may wing their interviews, asking completely different questions of various candidates, making it difficult to compare them to each other.

Unfortunately, you don't know what biases your interviewer may bring to your interview. There are, however, several things that you can do to help minimize biases and increase your chances of being selected for a job. Although even doing these four things is no guarantee that you will get the job, I can promise you that it will increase your chances considerably. These are all common-sense things to do, but you would be surprised how many people don't do them.

1. Go to the interview prepared. There is no excuse for going to an interview unprepared. Here are some things you can do to be prepared for any interview:

a. Be thoroughly familiar with everything on your résumé, and be prepared to answer questions about the information on your résumé.

b. Research the company you're interviewing with. When I was employment manager, earlier in my career, I would always ask candidates to tell me what they knew about our company. I was surprised at the number of candidates who knew very little about the company and who obviously made no effort to look at the company's press releases or annual report. All this information is easily available on the Internet today, so there is no reason you should ever go to an interview without a good knowledge of the company you're interviewing with. Interviewers will be impressed if you've done your homework about their company.

c. Try to find out as much as you can about the position you're interviewing for. This information might also be available on the Internet, or the company might be willing to give you a job description before the interview.

Information is powerful and will give you an opportunity to make sure you're interested in and qualified for the position, as well as help you sell yourself as the right person for the job.

d. If you know someone who works for the company, talk to them before your interview. Employees of the company may provide you valuable insights into the company's philosophy, culture, competition, products, and other important information. This person might also be able to provide a recommendation or to put in a good word for you.

2. Hone your interviewing skills. Interviewing for a job isn't something people do routinely, so the better prepared you are for the interview, the greater your chances are of getting the job. The best way to practice for an interview is to get someone you know to role-play an interview with you. Better yet, get several people to role-play with you and then ask them to provide an honest critique of how you did. I suggest that you even dress for the role-play as you would for the interview. Ask the person playing the interviewer to give you some candid feedback about how you look. The interviewer should be provided with a list of questions to ask you that will allow you to practice your answers. A list of commonly asked interview questions is provided later in this chapter.

3. Videotape your practice interview sessions. Yes, it's painful to watch yourself on video, but videos don't lie. All great athletes videotape and watch their performances. They and their coaches will go over the videos in excruciating detail looking for what the athlete didn't do well in hopes of finding areas for improvement. The video will reveal things—both good and bad—about your interview style that you never knew. I've had people watch themselves on video and discover that they looked at the floor whenever they answered a question or that they crossed their arms, had a nervous twitch, or said "uh" constantly when answering questions—or that they never smiled. They would never have known about these negative verbal and nonverbal habits unless someone pointed them out to them or they saw them on tape.

Once you know the areas in which you need to improve your interviewing techniques, practice the correct technique until you master it. Don't assume that simply because you know it, you will correct it. Old habits are hard to break, but they can be broken—by practice. After you've practiced the new behaviors, go through the interview role-play again on tape and check the tape to see how much you've improved.

4. Before the interview, try to find out who you will be interviewing with and in what order. Your first interview may be a screening interview with someone from the

Human Resources department. This is a great opportunity to learn more about the position and about what they are looking for in the ideal candidate.

If you do well here, you will most likely be asked to return at a later date for an interview with one or more management-level people. These interviews are often a series of several back-to-back interviews with various people. Normally, the last person in the interview chain is the hiring decision maker, but not always. If at all possible, try to get an advance copy of your interview schedule, including the names and titles of people you will talk to during your interviews. This will help you know what to expect during the interviews and will give you a chance to perhaps find out information about these individuals by checking the company's Web site, reports, and press releases. The more information you know before the interview, the better prepared for it you will be.

Interviewing Well

When you've properly prepared yourself for the interview, you significantly increase your chances of doing well during the interview process. Being prepared before the interview also increases your confidence level. Here are some pointers to help the interviews go in your favor.

1. Get to the interview early. Make sure you arrive

early for the interview and allow time for traffic problems or other delays. If you've never been to the location before, scout it out the day or evening before the interview so you know where to go and where to park.

2. Bring your résumé to the interview. It's always a good practice to bring several copies of your résumé with you to the interview. If you were asked to e-mail or fax your résumé to the company, the copy they have can be replaced by the professional one you brought to the interview. If you're not asked to provide your résumé during the interview, try to leave a copy with the person you're interviewing with.

3. Be yourself during the interview. Sure, you want to improve your interviewing skills (as we discussed earlier), but you always want to be yourself. Don't try to be someone you're not. You may be a quiet and somewhat reserved individual, and that's fine. You can be true to yourself and still be energetic and excited about the job possibility. If you exhibit no energy, passion, or excitement about the job, you hurt your chances of getting hired. Being quiet and reserved shouldn't be a crutch for not being friendly and energetic. Energy and enthusiasm are contagious, as are a friendly greeting and warm smile. Be careful not to talk too much during the interview. Don't start rambling while answering questions. You should talk about 60 to 70 percent of the time.

4. Look the part. Your appearance is part of your personal brand. Being well dressed and well groomed will enhance your chances of being hired. That why it helps to know the organization's culture and standards. If the written or unwritten dress code is a business suit or dress and you show up in casual attire, you're off to a rough start before you say the first word. To compound the situation, you just put on yourself the stress of feeling as if you've blown it before you've gotten out of the starting gate. Today many large organizations (and most small ones) are business casual and have fairly relaxed dress codes, but it's always better to err toward being overdressed rather than underdressed. If you're wearing a business suit and the people you're interviewing with are dressed casually, it won't be a strike against you, but I can almost assure you that if it's the other way around, it will be.

5. Have a list of prepared questions you want to ask during or at the conclusion of each interview. At the end of most interviews, the interviewer will ask if you have any questions you want to ask. After reviewing the company's material, make a list of questions about the industry, company, and job you want to know more about. Having a written list of good questions shows the interviewer that you're interested, organized, and prepared. Not asking questions leaves the interviewer thinking that you're not very interested in the company. I find that it makes a good impression to ask the interviewer about his or her career with the company. Most people like to talk about themselves and their careers, and asking about them shows that you're interested in their background and opinions. Here are a few good questions to ask the interviewer:

- How long have you been with XYZ Company?
- What has been your career path within XYZ Company?
- What are the top two or three reasons you enjoy working here?
- I noticed in your last annual report that the company was (expanding, developing new products, implementing new systems, etc.); how is (whatever issue you pick) progressing?

6. Discern what type of person, skills, and experiences your interviewers are looking for and tailor your answers to meet their needs. During your interview, sell your strengths and experiences as they relate to what they are seeking in the ideal candidate. For example, if you're an engineer and it's obvious they're looking for someone with strong project management skills and expertise—and you have these skills—then emphasize these qualities in your answers. Don't be talking about how great you are at engineering design or estimating if that's not what they're really looking for.

7. Be honest and candid with your answers. If you're asked something you don't know the answer to, tell the interviewer you don't know rather than trying to make up some answer or pretend to know more about something than you really do. The interviewer will appreciate your honesty. Most good interviewers can see through a candidate who is winging it or making something up.

8. In your mind, have your own agenda and know what key selling points you want to make. You know better than anyone else what your strengths are; try to play to those during the interview. If asked about something that forces you to provide a negative, be honest but use the technique of redirection to get back to your agenda and selling points. Let's say that the interviewer asks you how much salary you made in your last position and you tell him. If he responds, "That's more than we can pay you in the job we're talking about," you have a opportunity to redirect the question. If you're honestly willing to work for less money, you can redirect by saying, "I appreciate that this position doesn't pay as much as my last job. But salary isn't my most important priority. I'm much more concerned about being in a position where I can be valued, have an opportunity to contribute to the success of the organization, and continue to learn new things and grow professionally or technically. I've learned that if I continue to do those things well each day, the salary will take care of itself over time." Such an answer turns what could have been a negative in the eyes of an interviewer into a positive, taking the focus off salary and shifting it to contribution to the organization.

9. **Conclude each interview on a positive note.** At the conclusion of each interview, be sure to thank the interviewer for his or her time and explain that you're very interested in becoming part of the organization and that you look forward to hearing from him or her soon.

10. **Be prepared for the questions an interviewer may ask you during the interview.** Most interviewers, if they are trained and experienced, will have a standard set of interview questions targeted at answering two broad questions. First, *can* you do the job (based on your skills and abilities)? Second, *will* you do the job (based on your behavior, corporate fit, and career aspirations)? An interviewer should only ask you questions related to the job for which you are interviewing. Here is a list of commonly asked questions during interviews. Note most questions will be opened-ended questions, unable to be answered with a yes or no, to give you a chance to elaborate in your answers.

* *Tell me about yourself.*

It is estimated that 80 percent of job interviews begin with this simple question, but many candidates, unprepared for this question, hurt themselves by rambling on for fifteen minutes, going over their entire life story or delving into unnecessary personal history. Instead, be prepared to answer by starting with the present, explaining why you are qualified for the position. (Never forget during the interview that you must sell what the buyer is buying.) This is the most important consideration when job hunting.

* *Tell me about your past jobs.*
* *Why are you interested in the job here at*
  XYZ Company?
* *Why do you want to leave your current job?*

(Don't be negative when discussing your past employer or employers.)

* *What is the ideal job for you?* (This gives you a great chance to tailor your answer to what they're looking for in the ideal candidate.)
* *What do you enjoy most* (and least) *about your*
  current job?
* *What type of environment do you enjoy working in?*
* *What do you consider your top three strengths*
  and weaknesses?

- Tell me about some of your major accomplishments in your past jobs.
- Tell me about any experiences, both positive and negative, you've had while working on a team or in a team environment.
- I notice that you are no longer employed. Why did you leave your last job?
- How do you define success?
- What are your career goals? What do you hope to be doing in five years? Ten years?
- Is there anything that would prevent you from working the hours we require for this job?
- Is there anything that would prevent you from traveling if the job required it?
- Describe your working relationship with your previous supervisor. (Don't criticize your boss.)
- How do your peers describe you?
- Why should we hire you?
- What motivates you from a work perspective?
- How well do you think you handle organizational change, and why?
- What new skills do you want to learn?

If you're interviewing for a management job, you may be asked other questions:

- How do you describe your leadership style?
- What skills and abilities do you think a good supervisor needs to have to be successful?
- Tell about the toughest management problem you've had to handle.
- Tell me about any experience you've had in implementing major organizational changes.
- How would you handle such and such a situation (a hypothetical situation such as firing someone or seeing someone do something unethical)?

Although these are common questions asked during interviews, I'm surprised at how many people aren't prepared to answer them or give some rambling answer. If you know before your interview at least 90 percent of what you will be asked, there is no reason you shouldn't be prepared. Take the time to think through each of these interview questions, and write down your responses to each question. Work on making your responses positive, clear, concise, and brief. The interviewers will be evaluating you on how well you communicate and think on your feet. If you've practiced responding to these questions in advance, it will work to your advantage and give you added confidence going into your interview. You don't want your responses to sound rehearsed, but you don't want to stumble around trying to find a good response, either. On questions where you want to include several points in your answer, because

Lubbock Public Library

User name: RATLIFF, GARY LAWRENCE

Item ID: 50578U1764523q
Title: Poised for success : mastering th
e four qualities
Date due: 12/11/2012,23:59

Item ID: 627721
Title: Surviving and thriving after losi
ng your job : ho
Date due: ~~12/4/2012,23:59~~

5/18/12

Thank you for supporting
your public libraries!
Check us out online at:
www.lubbocklibrary.com

you've already thought through your answers and crafted responses, you can be more targeted in your answers. For example, imagine you are asked, "What are your strengths?" Let's say you know you want to highlight three specific strengths. A great communicator would answer by saying, "I believe I have three primary strengths. The first strength is . . . . The second strength is . . . . My third and final strength is . . . . The interviewer will be impressed that you knew before answering that you had three strengths and could precisely articulate what they were.

Once you've refined your answers, read over them several times daily until they become ingrained in your memory. It's not important that you be able to answer the questions verbatim; continually reviewing the questions and answers will make you able to respond when asked in an articulate manner. The key is practice, practice, and more practice.

What to Do After the Interview is Over

The outcome of the interview is largely out of your hands at this point. There is one thing, however, you can still do to enhance your chances and keep your name in front of the prospective employer. It's important that you ask each person with whom you interview for one of his or her business cards. The card will give you his or her correct title and mailing address and make it possible for you to contact him or her in the future as part of your networking activities if you don't get the job.

The day immediately following your interview, send a handwritten thank-you note to everyone who interviewed you. Be sure to send it the next day, because it will take a couple of days to be delivered. Handwritten notes make a more positive impression than e-mails. A handwritten note is considered a nice, thoughtful touch and is another opportunity to keep your name in their minds.

After the interview is over, back at your home or hotel room, take a few minutes to critique how well you did. I suggest you take a page in your journal and draw a line down the middle of the page, creating two columns. Label the left-hand column "What Went Well" and the right-hand column "What I Need to Improve." Then, in each column, honestly and objectively assess how well you did during the interview. Begin to develop a written plan to improve each item you listed in the right-hand column. If you don't get the job, you will have better prepared yourself for your next interview by having fine-tuned specific areas in need of improvement. Repeat this process after *every* job interview—it will pay great dividends in the long run.

If you don't get a certain job, it's fine to be disappointed; that's to be expected. Learn from your experience and move on. Each step you take moves you closer to your objective: finding a new job, starting a new business, or whatever else you've decided to do with your new career.

How to Use Your Network

Did you know you have a network? You do. In fact, everyone does. The only difference is the size of each person's network. Your primary network is made up of the people you know: what some people refer to as your sphere of influence. Your secondary network is made up of the people known by the people in your primary network. Your tertiary network is the people known by the people in your secondary network—and it just keeps going.

The following diagram is a picture of your primary, secondary, and tertiary networks. You are the center circle. The next circle is your primary network, the next circle your secondary, and the last your tertiary.

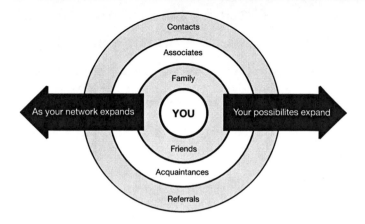

Networking is your chief route to finding another job. It is believed that at least 60 percent—perhaps up to 90 percent—of all jobs are found through networking. Clearly, networking should be the major focus of your job marketing campaign. Begin by making a list of everyone you know—people within your primary sphere of influence. Write their names in your journal and group them into five categories:

1. **Family members**
2. **Friends**
3. **Associates** (coworkers and people from organizations or associations you belong to or have belonged to who know you).
4. **Acquaintances** (people who know you and who will immediately recognize your name, and people you knew or were friends with in the past but haven't talked to in a number of years).
5. **Contacts** (people you've met in the past but whom you don't know very well and who may or may not remember you—most likely people you may have exchanged business cards with or met briefly at meetings or events).

I suggest that when compiling your list you make four columns on each sheet of paper. The first column will be your list of names. Leave several lines of space between each name; better yet, dedicate a page in your journal to each person in your network. Why this is important will become clearer later in this section.

How many names are on your list? Let's assume that forty people compose your primary network. This is the group with whom you will start networking, beginning with family and working your way down through all the names in your contacts category. This is the power of networking: if you know forty people, each of whom knows another forty people, your direct and secondary networks have now expanded to over sixteen hundred people. You have just exponentially expanded your network, and thus your chances of finding someone who knows about a job that *you* will end up filling.

Time to Start Networking

Once you've written down your list of contacts in your journal, you're well on your way. Ask your spouse or other family members to look at your list; they will likely add several names you missed on your first pass. Put these additional people in the appropriate category, and we'll move on to the next important step.

You need to determine how you're going to approach each person in your network: what you're going to say to them and what you're going to ask them to do to help you. Let's begin by developing our networking spiel, or message. The spiel will work whether you contact someone by phone, e-mail, or letter. Your spiel is similar to a stump speech used by campaigning politicians. Good politicians know the three or four key points they want to make when given the opportunity.

Your sample spiel

Name, (*Preface this with "Dear" if you're sending a letter.*)

I hope things are well with you. (*If this is a family member, friend, or other person who knows you well or fairly well, it's good to expand this section to make it more personal.*)

I'm looking for another job, and I would greatly appreciate any help you can give me. My goal is to secure a (job title or type) position with a (company name or industry type) company. I would appreciate any job leads, career advice, or other thoughts you might have that would help me with my search. Also, if you're not aware of any leads at this time but know someone who might be able to help me out with leads or other helpful information, would you mind providing me with their name and contact information?

Thanks in advance for any help, advice, or other contacts you can provide me. I'll give you a call in the next week to touch base with you. I look forward to talking with you, and I appreciate your time and help.

Sincerely,

Your name

Your contact information

Communicating with Your Network

You will need to think about how best to communicate with each person on your network list. Most people use e-mail today, but some people may not, making a letter or phone call the best way to contact those individuals. E-mail allows you to contact several people simultaneously and to get quick feedback, but the downside of e-mail is its impersonality—and many people are already overloaded with e-mails. If you choose to send mass e-mails to people in your network, be sure to put all recipients' addresses in the bcc—blind copy—field, because some people don't like to have their e-mail addresses shared with people they don't know.

You will need to develop a system to help you track the

status of your networking activities so that you can know where you stand with each person on your list, as well as any commitments you've made to people in your network—or that they've made to you. As you talk to people in your network, be sure to keep good notes. If someone in your network tells you about a job lead or mentions another person you should contact, it won't do you any good if you can't find that person's name or phone number when you need it. I highly recommend that you get all your networking notes in one place—in a journal, a binder, a notebook, a planner, a day timer, or in whatever other system works best for you. You will be talking to a lot of people and taking pages of notes that you will be referring to throughout your job search. Sticky notes or random slips of paper lack the organization you will need to stay on top of your networking activities and can be easily misplaced or lost. The other nice thing about a self-contained system such as a journal is that you can carry it with you wherever you go. If you get a call while sitting in a restaurant, coffee shop, or just about any other place, you can record your conversation in your system while it's still fresh in your mind.

Some people like to use a PDA or PC, both of which are powerful tools but are hard to carry with you all the time. Another downside of a PC is that it has to be up and run-

Sample networking page from my journal

Name	Contacted	Follow-up	Status
Tom Williams Friend 555-2323 patwill@e-mail.com	June 8	June 15	Didn't know of any jobs. Suggested I call Mason Lackey, President Lackey Contractors 555-8889. Tom said he might have one more name for me in a few days.
		June 23	Call Tom to check on the person he was thinking about referring me to.

Name	Contacted	Follow-up	Status
Mason Lackey (Referred by Tom Williams) President Lackey Construction 555-8889	June 10		Sent e-mail to Mason. Waiting to hear back from him.

ning in order to make notes in it. A journal or notebook simply requires a quick flip to the last page of notes. It's simple, effective, mobile, and fast. One good use of the PC in networking is to keep an Excel spreadsheet of your networking activities and progress. I find it best to use a journal to record notes and commitments in during the day, then update the Excel spreadsheet in the evening. The spreadsheet also provides a backup should you lose your notebook—something I don't recommend!* Here's a simple way to organize your journal so you can keep track of your networking activities:

In this example, anything highlighted in yellow is a "to-do" activity requiring action on your part. As you flip through the pages of your system, you can quickly see anything requiring action on your part. Once an action is completed, simply draw a line through it.

The key to effective networking is to be persistent and relentless. You may not be comfortable calling or even e-mailing people you don't know very well to ask for help. My advice to you is to move beyond the fear of being rejected or of inconveniencing someone. Force yourself to make the calls and the contacts. People will not mind helping you if they can, but they can't help you if you don't ask.

> *If you never ask, the answer is always the same—no.*

People on your network list will fall into one of three categories:

---

*An Excel spreadsheet can be downloaded from the resources section of my Web site, www.davidjonesgroupllc.com to help you track and manage your networking.

1. **Uncontacted**: These are people you haven't contacted yet but plan to contact soon.
2. **Contacted Hot**: These are people you have contacted who gave you a name to contact or a possible job lead or who are thinking about it and who will get in touch with you should they think of anything or anyone who could help you.
3. **Contacted Cold**: These are people you have contacted who weren't able to help you.

Following up is an essential part of networking. Many of the people you contact may not be able to help you immediately. They may need to think about people they know whom you should consider contacting, or perhaps a job they know about slips their mind during your initial contact with them. Make it one of your behaviors to follow up with everyone who is "contacted hot" in your network at least every two weeks, even if they said they would contact you. Never assume they will get back in touch with you. They may forget to call you back with a name or potential job lead, and if they don't hear from you in several weeks, they might think that you've found a job and feel no reason to contact you. Contact them to see if they have thought of anyone they can refer you to or if they've heard of any jobs that could have opened up since you last talked. It can be a short two- or three-minute phone call.

You should also follow up on everyone on your list who is "contacted cold" at least monthly. A lot can happen in four weeks; they may have thought of someone you should talk to, or they might now know of a job opening you should pursue. If they do give you a referral or job lead, change their status to "contacted hot" and follow up with them in two weeks. When you follow up with them, let them know how much you appreciate their help, and update them on the status of their referral or lead. Following up often yields additional referrals and leads.

The secret to networking is to always look for opportunities to expand the list of names on your network list, keeping as many people as possible marked "contacted hot." Keep reminding yourself as you network that each contact takes you one step closer to finding the job you desire.

Expanding Your Network

Obviously, the more names on your network list, the better off you are. Look for opportunities to expand your list. Take advantage of opportunities to meet people in social settings—at your kids' school or athletic events, at church, or at any other place where you're around people. I heard of someone who was looking for a job who made it a habit to go to Starbucks® each day for an hour or two to make phone calls or to send e-mails. While standing in line to order his coffee or while sitting at one of the tables, he struck up conversations with those in line or with those sitting next to him. He said that a few of those conversations led to good job leads he wouldn't have known about had he not purposefully worked to get them. He looked for every opportunity to expand his network list and use it to his advantage.

Once you find a job, it's good to let the people on your network list know. It's a way to bring closure as well as to tell them how much you appreciated their help, letting them know that you will be more than glad to return the favor if ever they need your help.

Get networking cards printed

Before you start networking, one of the best investments you can make is to get networking cards professionally printed. Your networking card is actually nothing more than a business card that contains your name and contact information. As you meet people, look for opportunities to exchange cards with them. Each time you exchange cards, you've just expanded the size of your network. Some of the people you meet may think of a job lead or referral to give you in the days or weeks after they talk with you but won't know how to get in touch with you. Your networking card solves that problem for them, and every time they come across it, it keeps your name in front of them. You can even order free cards at www.vistaprint.com.

Employment Advertising

Other sources of potential jobs are advertisements placed in newspapers and trade journals and on the Internet. Part of the plan you developed earlier should include regularly checking these sources and applying for any jobs that meet your search criteria. Most major newspapers and trade journals can be viewed online today, making it easier for you to monitor their job ads on a weekly basis, if not even more frequently. Your local library may also subscribe to some of larger national newspapers. Remember—the job search experts recommend that you look at employment ads at night, reserving your day for more important activities, such as interviewing and networking.

A number of Internet sites now carry employment ads online. You can also put your résumé online at sites like Monster.com and CareerBuilder.com™ after setting up a free account that allows potential employers to scout you out. Monster® will even notify you by e-mail as job matches are posted. You should consider using Internet sites like these as part of your search process. But don't rely solely on employment ads to find work. Remember that most jobs are found through networking. Networking must be your first area of focus in your job search.

Search Firms

There are a variety of employment search firms you should consider in your job search, depending on your job level. Generally, employment search firms fall into three categories:

1. Temporary Employment Agencies: These agencies work with their client companies to provide employees on a temporary basis. Sometimes a company has to temporarily backfill a position while an employee is out sick, on vacation, or on maternity or paternity leave. However, many times a company is looking for someone to temporarily backfill a job opening while the company looks for someone to permanently fill it. Companies typically use temporary employees for non–supervisory level positions—both professional and nonprofessional. Many times the people who fill these positions on a temporary basis end up getting the job full-time. You may want to consider pursuing this job route if you need to find other work quickly after losing your job, even if it's on a temporary basis, to keep earning some income while you continue your job search. One advantage of working as a temporary is that it gives you a chance to evaluate the company and allows them to evaluate you at the same time. Should they offer you the job on a full-time basis, you will already have some understanding of the company, its culture, and the job requirements before accepting their offer, which increases your chances of finding a good job fit.

2. **Contingency search firms:** These firms usually specialize in placing professional and management level employees. An organization hires them to find a specific type of individual and pays them a percentage of the employee's annual salary as their fee only after the person is hired. The fee is contingent on the person's being hired. If the search firm submits several candidates and none of them get hired, then no fee is paid. Contingency search firms have an extensive database of potential applicants who have supplied them with résumés. You should approach contingency search firms in your area and meet with them to let them know what type of work you're looking for and to provide them with a copy of your résumé. You never know when they will have a job pop up on their radar screen for which you are an excellent match.

3. **Executive search firms:** These firms tend to specialize

in highly technical individual contributor positions, in certain industries, or in executive-level positions only. Some executive search firms only do searches for candidates at a minimum salary level of $100,000. Executive search firms are approached by a client to do a targeted job search. They are paid a certain percentage of the position's annual salary and bonus whether or not the company actually hires one of the firm's candidates. If you're at the executive level, you should contact any executive search firms you know of or have worked with in the past that specialize in your industry or that could possibly help you in your job search. It's always good to have a few executive-level headhunters as part of your network.

The following is an interview with Steve Hayes. Steve is the founder and senior partner of the Human Capital Group, a successful executive search firm based in Franklin, Tennessee.

DJ: *Steve, tell me about your firm.*

SH: We are a retained global executive search firm hired by our clients to find a needle in a haystack. We specialize in finding mid-to-senior-level executives.

DJ: *Your firm, to my knowledge, is unique in that you have based your firm's values on biblical principles. What is the reason you've chosen to do this?*

SH: We've actually chosen business principles and defined them with scripture. We have selected core guiding principles of focus, leadership, respect, and integrity. We have taken those principles and defined them, in our estimation, by the best leader historically and sustainably—Jesus Christ. We decided about three years ago, after much discussion internally, along with some external advice to the contrary, that this was the right thing for our company to do. We did lose a few clients by doing so, but we've also been immensely blessed. These guiding principles are there simply to make sure we hold ourselves accountable for doing them.

DJ: *When someone comes to your firm asking for your help in finding a job, what do you tell them, and how does your company go about helping them?*

SH: We do have a lot of people contact us and ask for our help. We have made a commitment to ourselves that we will take thirty minutes out of our busy schedule to talk to each of them. In doing this, we know that only 1 in 200 of those people will find a job through our firm. We view this as a way of tithing our time. When we talk to them, we try to ask probing questions and encourage them to make sure they are focused on what's important in their lives. We try to get them to evaluate their values in life and factor those into their career decision. I know that's important, because I came to that reality myself several years ago. I had a goal to be the top HR person in a Fortune 100 company. I was tracking along nicely to achieve that goal, but it was taking a toll on my wife and my five kids. We had moved eight times in a relatively short time span, and the kids were constantly in different schools. In a discussion with my wife, I realized I was serving the wrong board of directors. I was trying to please my corporate board when my real board should be my family, with God as my chairman. I decided to leave my corporate job and start my own business so I could spend more time with my family. I don't regret that decision. Each person needs to define who and what are his or her board of directors and definition of success.

DJ: *In working with corporate clients, what is your view of job security in the corporate world in the Twenty-first Century?*

SH: True job security as we once knew it no longer exists. We're all free agents now. Corporations are under tremendous pressure to perform and to improve their numbers monthly and quarterly. The irony is, shareholders— individuals like you and me—buy and sell stocks based on how well a company is performing and what is its potential. We help create the pressure on companies to perform. Employees should not entrust their careers to their bosses. It's your career; you own it and are responsible for it. You need to see if your company is investing in your growth and development. If not, you may be better off working somewhere else. With all the changes in the corporate world today, employees, at some point in their careers, will be looking for another job. It's not a matter of "if," but "when."

DJ: *When you work with people who have been fired, what emotional struggles do you most often see?*

SH: We see the full range of emotions—fear, anger, low self-esteem, embarrassment, and depression. Those are normal and expected reactions to being fired. The sooner they can move through those emotions and accept what has happened to them, the better. It doesn't help them to be looking for a job or interviewing and come across as stewing in all the negative things that have happened. We help them to focus on the positive things. After being fired, they do have a job. That job is to find a new job.

DJ: *More employees are losing their jobs because of mergers, acquisitions, downsizings, etc. What can employees do to prepare themselves for the possibility of being let go by their employers?*

SH: They need to think of themselves as being self-employed. They need to have career dreams and goals. As I said earlier, they need to figure out which board of directors they want to work for. They shouldn't wait for some transition to start preparing themselves. They should be preparing themselves now.

DJ: *You help your clients prepare their résumés. Any advice for people and what mistakes do you most often see in résumés?*

SH: The one thing I see most lacking in résumés are results. The businesses and executives I'm working for are all results-oriented. That's what they look for in résumés: *what has a person accomplished?* When someone lists a bunch of responsibilities but not accomplishments, their value plummets. They need to remember—they are selling themselves. They should make sure there are no gaps in their employment history. Gaps are red flags, and I always look for gaps. I tell people to be honest about their journey. Other red flags are typos, insufficient results, and limited contact information.

DJ: *What are some of the keys to successful interviews?*

SH: The most important thing is be yourself. Don't try to be someone you're not or try to be who you think the hiring authority wants you to be. If you're not yourself in the interview, they are going to figure it out sooner or later. Also, make sure you're prepared to answer any questions you're asked about your résumé. I encourage my clients to practice interviewing. Interviewing for a job isn't something people do that often. It's helpful to get someone to role-play with you so they can critique how you do. It also doesn't hurt to tape or videotape your role-play session and then watch it. You may be surprised at some things you see yourself do on tape. There is a reason professional athletes and coaches tape games and then carefully review them. It allows them to see what they did well and where they need to improve. When I submit my top ten candidates to a client, I know only one of them will get the job; all the others will be disappointed, and I have to relay the bad news to them. I tell them not to view it as rejection, but as God's protection. He has something else in store for them.

DJ: *Steve, do you have any other thoughts or suggestions you can offer people?*

SH: I encourage people to invest in themselves. They need to exercise and take care of themselves physically, emotionally, and spiritually. If a person is out of shape or overweight, the person doing the hiring may think, "Why should I expect this person to take care of my business when he or she doesn't take care of themselves?" When looking for a job, networking is critically important. They need to knock on as many doors as they can. Even when they find a job, they should continue networking. The statistics I've seen indicate that 90 percent of all jobs are filled through networking. Find ways to stay in touch with people in your network. You need to keep your name, which is your brand, in front of them as much as possible. You have a circle of influence; use it.

Outplacement Firms

Many organizations—particularly larger corporations —use outplacement firms when they are reducing staff. Many of these firms offer a broad range of services to assist employees in their search for meaningful jobs and careers. Outplacement firms typically offer organizations two types of outplacement services. The first is group classes and the second is individual services. Let's look at each type of service.

Group outplacement

When an organization is reducing staff, it may engage the services of an outplacement firm to help the severed employees transition from being employed to looking for another job. The outplacement firm is hired by the organization to provide group sessions or workshops to the terminated employees immediately after being informed that they no longer have a job. The terminated employees are usually asked to go to a conference room at their work location or an offsite meeting room at a nearby hotel, where they meet with counselors from the outplacement firm. The purpose of the initial meeting is to help employees deal with the shock of having just been terminated, to provide an opportunity for them to vent their frustration and anger, and to learn about the services (usually group workshops) that the firm is providing to them in order to help them successfully transition to other employment. Depending on what the organization arranges with the outplacement firm, it usually conducts a workshop with small groups of terminated employees that cover four specific areas:

1. Understanding the dynamics of change and dealing with the emotions of losing a job, coping with the stress, communicating with family and friends, and keeping the right attitude while going forward.
2. Assessing the past by providing various personality testing instruments and career interest inventories coupled with identifying personal needs, values, interests, skills, and accomplishments.
3. Developing tools to help employees in their job searches. These include designing résumés, developing a list of references, writing cover letters, and using a system to track it all.
4. Implementing strategies and techniques to help them in their job quest. This may include scanning the marketplace, targeting specific companies, developing a contact or network list, setting career goals, learning about effective interviewing, and negotiating an offer.

If your company offers you group outplacement services, I encourage you to use them. Outplacement firms specialize in helping people like you transition to other jobs or even to other careers. They are very experienced and in tune with the marketplace and know which job search techniques work and which ones don't. The workshops also give you a chance to be around other coworkers, and probably some friends, who find themselves in the same boat you're in, as well as to support each other through a difficult time.

Individual outplacement

Because individual outplacement is expensive, it is usually limited to management- and executive-level employees. Individual outplacement can last for months and includes many of the same topics covered in group outplacement, but the outplacement is normally conducted one-on-one with a professional from the outplacement firm. Furthermore, individual outplacement can include other services such as spousal relocation programs, executive coaching, financial planning, and career center services. The outplacement services may also provide use of a career management center that includes office space, telephones, computers, research material, and other services to assist people in their job searches.

Most management- and executive-level employees find individual outplacement very helpful in their searches for new jobs. If you're eligible for individual outplacement services, you should definitely check it out to see whether you want to take advantage of it. It's a good idea to meet with the outplacement firm to see what services they can provide you and to get your questions answered.

The following is an interview with Dennis Russell, who has over twenty years of experience in providing outplacement services to thousands of clients via his firm, Russell Reynolds, located in Brentwood, Tennessee.

DJ: *Tell me about Russell Reynolds: what services does your firm provide?*

DR: Our company is broader than just outplacement, since we do some executive search, training, and coaching, but our primary focus is outplacement. We do different types of outplacement ranging from executive to group outplacement. Through our partner program, we have access to over two hundred other outplacement firms across the world.

DJ: *Who uses outplacement services like yours?*

DR: Our programs range from one-on-one executive programs to time-sensitive programs where a company can select a program that might last a few weeks or a couple of days. We are often asked to do one- or two-day seminars for groups, usually ten to fifteen hourly or nonexempt employees at a time, whereas executive programs are more extensive and can last for months.

DJ: *What are the two or three most important things people need to be doing immediately after being terminated?*

DR: The first couple of things we advise people on are how to communicate what has happened to them to family, friends, and associates, and how to organize themselves. We ask them to tell us about themselves and their families. We can then better instruct them on how to communicate what has happened to them to their families, and how to solicit their support. You don't walk in the house and say, "I had a great day at the office, except for getting fired." For example, if a person who has just been fired has a junior in high school, the teenager's concern will be, *Are we going to have to relocate?* The wife will have a different set of concerns. We urge people to be open and honest and to tell their family as soon as possible what has happened in as positive a manner as possible. We recognize that being positive may be difficult to do, but it's important to remain positive and look for the silver lining in the cloud. We remind our clients that they were looking for a job when they got the last one. Also, leaving a company now forces them to look at other things and gives them an opportunity to possibly pursue a career they've thought about but didn't have the courage to do because it would have required quitting their jobs.

Organizing themselves simply means getting together information about themselves—which they need to use in constructing their résumés—and about their interests and people they know. It's good for them to keep a pad of paper with them at all times and write down the names of people they know or come into contact with who can help them with their job search. We instruct them to organize this information either manually or electronically, since it will serve as the basis for their networking.

DJ: *You work with companies all across the country. How has job security changed over the last twenty years—or has it?*

DR: Statistics I've seen indicate that today the average college graduate will have three to four careers and seven to eight jobs. A high-school graduate or technical-school graduate is predicted to have five to six careers and eight to eleven jobs. The lifespan of a good company today averages around forty years. So if someone goes to work at a company that has been in business for thirty years, they shouldn't expect to be at that company for many years or to retire there, because the company probably won't be in business that long. I suggest people take a presidential approach to a particular job. When a person becomes President of the United States, he or she can only expect to be in that job for four years, or possibly eight years, but no longer. That's a great mindset to take into any new job. Then you're not surprised or totally disappointed if you lose your job or the company folds down the road. Change is inevitable.

DJ: *When working with people who have just been fired, what emotions do you see them most often struggle with?*

DR: We often see people go through all the steps of what's called the grief cycle, which ranges from denial to acceptance. We remind them, when they get to the acceptance stage, it doesn't mean they agree with what has happened to them. You may not ever agree with what the company did to you, but you've accepted it and you're ready to move on. One thing you see many people struggle with is self-doubt, even if their company just let hundreds or even thousands of employees go. Some people want to personalize their firing and struggle to get past *Why me?* They keep thinking, *Did I do something wrong? Should I have done something differently?* The anger stage is usually short-lived, and it can be channeled into positive activity, like networking. Another thing we work with people on is when they are about to get a job offer, not to stop their networking and job search activities. The job may not come to fruition, and if they stopped their search process, some people find it difficult to gear back up and start again. It's critical they keep the activity going should they not get the job. I remind them— Babe Ruth was one of the greatest home run hitters, but he also struck out more than anyone else in history. They have to keep swinging at the ball.

DJ: *How important is networking in finding another job?*

DR: The lowest number I have seen indicates 66 percent of all jobs are found through networking. The more senior the person is or the more limited they are in job scope or geography, the more likely they are to find a job through networking. Networking is absolutely critical and the key is to call back every two or three weeks to follow up on active leads. People on your list get busy and forget about you or think, *I haven't heard from him, so he must have found a job.* We find it's sometimes the third or fourth contact with a person on your list where a lead develops that results in the person finding a job. People should network during the day, when their contacts are at work and easy to reach. They should use the evening hours for reading job ads and doing online searches.

DJ: *How long does it take someone going through outplacement to usually find a job?*

DR: The old rule of thumb was that it takes one month for each $10,000 of salary to find a comparable job. I don't agree with that rule any more, because over the past decade or two, salaries have been inflated. We see it typically take a senior-level person six to nine months to find another position.

DJ: *With more and more employees losing their jobs because of mergers, acquisitions, downsizings, and so on, what can employees do to prepare themselves for possibly losing their jobs in the future?*

DR: It's important that employees keep learning and developing. They should take advantage of any training opportunity that comes their way and look for ways they can broaden their network through getting involved in professional or civic organizations.

DJ: *You help your clients prepare their résumés. What advice do you offer people on résumé preparation?*

DR: I sometimes have to remind them they aren't having mom read their résumés. Résumés should be as brief as possible. A one-page résumé is nice, but if someone has more than five to seven years of experience, they most likely will need a two-page résumé. It's important to emphasize your accomplishments more than your responsibilities. It's fine to have a line, or maybe two, to describe the job, but then they should bullet their accomplishments, special projects, or special skills. Put your most recent jobs first, and work back chronologically. If they are very experienced, they shouldn't put a lot of information about jobs they had longer than ten years ago or college information. Employers are more concerned about *What have you done recently?* If people have written articles or white papers or published things, we suggest they include that information in an addendum.

DJ: *What are some common mistakes you see in résumés?*

DR: We often see résumés with too much personal information or containing noncritical information. If someone is interviewing for an accounting director or manager job and their first job was associate accountant, they don't need to say much about the duties of an associate accountant. The hiring person is probably very familiar with what most associate accountants do. Instead, talk about your accomplishments.

DJ: *What can people do while being interviewed to improve their chances of getting a job?*

DR: First, they should view the interview as a sales call, not an inquisition. They are selling themselves and their abilities. But they need to be a good listener and try to pick up on what the hiring authority is really looking for. Then you can sell yourself as someone who can help meet their organizational needs. Second, be careful not to talk about your past failures or be negative about having lost a job. If losing a past job comes up in the interview, focus on the positive things you learned from that experience and how it's better prepared you for the job you're interviewing for.

CHAPTER NINE

A New Beginning

Every day is an opportunity to make a new happy ending.

AUTHOR UNKNOWN

A s you've read this book, if you haven't found a job yet, I'm confident you will. It's my hope that you find the exact job or new career you've always been looking for that's aligned with your life purpose. When you do, you will wish you had found it much sooner—losing your job may end up having been the best thing that could have happened to you. When you find your ideal job, you will look forward to going to work each day because you're doing the thing you love to do. Work becomes fun and enjoyable—it's no longer *work*. I like Richard Branson's viewpoint on work: "I don't think of work as work and play as play. It's all living," Branson says. Now, *there's* a guy who loves what he's doing each day. You're probably thinking, "If I was a billionaire with my own private island, like him, I would be as happy as Branson." However, if you've read Branson's autobiography, *Losing My Virginity,* you know that he didn't inherit his wealth. He earned it by pursing his passion, taking risks, and going broke numerous times—but never quitting or giving up on his dream.

As you transition to your new job or career, I hope you will learn from the experience and, as a result, grow both personally and professionally. I believe we learn more from our failures than we do from our successes. I have learned a lot about myself and others through the process of losing my job. Hopefully, you can say the same about yourself, and at the end of the process you, too, will have become a stronger person. As you begin your new job or career, it's a great opportunity to leverage what you've learned after losing your job to develop five new disciplines in your life. These disciplines will benefit you as you begin an entirely new chapter of your life. They will also help you prepare for future changes that may come your way, because even when you find a new job or career, there are no guarantees that it will work out the way you planned. Any of us could find ourselves going through the job search process again in the future. If that were to happen, as you incorporate these five disciplines into your life, you will be much better prepared for any future job or career changes.

1. Make Learning Continuous and a Habit

Our world is constantly changing, and the speed of the changes keeps increasing, propelled by technological advances. Just think of all the changes we have experienced in the last ten years—cell phones, PDAs, blogs, wikis, Google™, Web conferencing, YouTube, portable GPS, digital cameras, WANs, LANs, and the list goes on and on. Sometimes we would like to see all the technology slow down, but if we're going to thrive in this new world, we must learn to embrace it—to make learning continuous and a way of life. Learning didn't stop when we graduated from high school or college. Learning is a lifestyle, a decision all of us must make, if we are to continue to grow personally, professionally, emotionally, and spirtually. The moment we stop learning, the world will pass us by.

2. Develop a Personal Growth Plan

You may want to consider developing a personal growth plan. The plan should set some specific growth goals that you want to achieve over the next year. It might include reading one book a month on a subject you're not familiar with or that you want to know more about. It could be attending a night class at your local college or university or taking an online class. It could be learning to use some new software, joining a professional organization or business group to keep current with new developments and trends, or listening to self-development CDs in your car as you drive to work each day. The list of ways you can grow and develop is endless, and so are your opportunities. But, like everything else in life, it doesn't just happen. You need to develop a plan and then execute your plan. You must recognize and seize the opportunities that come your way.

3. Keep Networking

You've probably been told many times that it's not what you know but who you know that counts. There is a lot of truth to that statement. The more people in your network or sphere of influence, the more resources you have available to help you should you need to call upon them. I've never consciously worked to develop a personal network of contacts. I've simply made it a practice to always keep the business cards of people I've met over the years. Many years ago I bought a business-card holder to file all the business cards I collect. It's a simple, cheap, and effective way to keep and organize business cards. I also enter the information from the business cards into Microsoft® Office Contacts, which syncs with my BlackBerry®.

The reason I like to also keep the information electronically is that I have it with me all the time on my phone for instant access. The other advantage of keeping it electronically is that I can include additional information about the person in the notes section of the contact page. After I meet people, I take a few minutes each evening to input important information about them into the notes section of MS Contacts. You can accomplish the same thing by writing it on the back of their business card.

I try to capture information not found on a business card, like the names of their spouse and children, where they attended college, their hobbies and interests, and other valuable information. I've seen some of these people three or four years later at a conference or meeting and shocked them by asking about their children by name or inquiring about a specific hobby they enjoyed. They thought I had a photographic memory, but in fact I had taken two or three minutes to enter this information into Contacts after first meeting them. Having this information is also a great way to stay in touch with them. For example, if you meet someone and learn that one of his or her hobbies is fly fishing, anytime you come across a good article on fly fishing, you can send it to him or her. It's a thoughtful gesture, and it makes your name memorable.

I have two grown children, Josh and Kim, both of whom are in their mid-twenties and are just beginning their careers. I'm teaching both of them the art of networking, because I think it will help them in the future—particularly because experts predict that their generation will have eight to ten different *careers*, not jobs, in a lifetime.

4. *Think Like You're Working for Yourself*

If you go to work for a business or organization, you're an employee working for your employer. Even though you're working for someone else, who signs your paycheck, I suggest you adopt a different mindset about your employment. Don't think of yourself as an employee. Instead, think of yourself as the owner and president of your own firm, providing a specialized service or area of expertise—accounting, engineering, electric, administrative assistance—to your present employer (or better yet, client). Pretend that you're contracting your services to your client and that either you or your client has the right to terminate your services at any point. As president, you're responsible for your own firm's success or failure, as well as its ultimate destiny. You are free to take your services to other clients who will provide you with greater opportunities and challenges should you desire. As long as your client is engaging your services, you will do an excellent job, because you value the reputation of your firm.

The great thing about developing this mindset is that you don't become dependent on your employer. It's a subtle but powerful mind shift into believing that you have total ownership and responsibility for your career, no longer dependent upon someone else to control your destiny. When working for yourself, you begin to think about what you have to do to develop and broaden your skills and abilities rather than depending on someone else to do it for you. This mindset helps to keep you mentally sharp and focused, as well as prepared for the unexpected. After all, we can't predict the future, but we can be prepared for it to the best of our abilities.

5. Help Others Who Lose Their Jobs

I know that my sensitivity to others who lose their jobs is much greater today than it was before I lost my job. I feel their pain and want to help them get back on their feet if I can. Having gone through what they are experiencing, I can offer them some valuable insight and help them deal with the emotions and struggles they will face while being unemployed. I now make a concerted effort to reach out to those people I know who are terminated, and I trust that you will do the same. When I was unemployed, I found that being able to talk to other people who had been down the road ahead of me was tremendously helpful and a great encouragement. I hope you will choose to adopt these five disciplines as you move forward.

What Direction will You Choose?

Life truly is a journey, and often its roads take us to places we never dreamed of or expected to ever be. Maybe your journey has brought you to a place you may have never been before. You find yourself standing at one of life's major intersections. The last few miles of your journey have taken you through some rough, curvy roads full of hills and valleys, often through fog and rain. It's a road you never traveled before, and you don't know what lies over the next hill or around the next curve—you're not even sure where the road goes.

You've come to a stop at a four-way intersection, and you have some choices to make about which way you'll travel. You know you've just come down a one-way road; you can't go back. You can only move forward on the journey.

Though surrounded by fog, you can see three roads signs at the intersection, each pointing to a different destination. You turn on your high beams, and suddenly, through the fog, you make out the faint outline of a town name and a historical roadside marker beside each road. You're all alone sitting at the intersection, so you get out of your vehicle and walk over to the road that goes to the left to read the sign.

The sign and marker says, "Defeatedville is a town that welcomes life's losers—those who have been knocked to the mat and don't want to get up and keep fighting. It's a place where the citizens wallow in self-pity and complain about being victims who have been treated unfairly. Few who choose to live here ever leave. It's not a happy town. There are no celebrations, and all the houses are dark and drab. It's a short distance to there from the intersection where you're standing, and the road is all downhill and smooth from here to there."

You backtrack across the intersection to the road that goes to the right and read its sign and marker. The marker says, "Sameville is a town that welcomes those who cherish the *status quo*. We don't like change in our town; things here are the same as they were the last time you may have passed through. Our citizens don't like to take risks, and we pride ourselves in rejecting progress and change. All the houses here look about the same, and we see no reason to change them. It's also a short distance from the intersection to our town, and the road is easy to travel."

You look around; you're still alone at the intersection, so you cut across a field to get to the last marker. As you approach it, you notice that it's called Opportunityville. The sign looks similar to the others, so you read it: "Opportunityville is a growing and exciting town, full of opportunities for all who venture here. We love and welcome change. We cherish new ideas and enjoy those who are willing to take risks and try new things. We believe in purpose-based living here; people who visit our town never leave. Our houses are unique and different, just as our citizens are. Our town is not the easiest to get to, and it's a longer journey. It requires you to travel over several mountains and some narrow roads that only the courageous can navigate; but once you arrive, you will find the journey to have been worth it."

You walk back to your car and note that there is still no one in sight. You have a decision you must make that no one can make for you—the road you will take. I hope you have the courage to drive straight ahead to Opportunityville. Don't take the easy roads to the right or the left. Although the road to Opportunityville takes more courage, it's worth the risk to those who choose to travel it. The decision you make about the road you will take will determine your destination and your future.

One Year Later

Ironically, as I write this chapter it's exactly one year to the day after leaving my corporate career with El Paso. I knew at that point that my long career was over and that I was standing at my own intersection. I, too, had to choose which direction I was going to go. I never considered the road to Defeatedville. It's simply not part of my DNA. It was narrowed down to two viable choices for me. I was never a big risk taker, and I found myself looking down the road toward Sameville. I had interviewed with a highly regarded firm who had offered me a good job. It was a nice, comfortable corporate job in a related industry. I confess that it was tempting financially—if I accepted the offer, I could pocket all my severance pay.

But I found myself also looking down the road toward Opportunityville. I had always dreamed of working for myself and starting my own business: now I had the opportunity to do it. But did I have the courage? Was I willing to take the risk? As I always do when faced with a major decision, I took out my journal and made a list of the pros and cons of accepting the job in hand and of starting my own company. My wife and I discussed the items on our list and prayed about it for several days. We didn't want to make the wrong decision. I was going through outplacement at the time and discussed it with my counselor, too.

I kept finding myself being drawn toward Opportunity-ville. I knew it was a riskier road for me to travel, but at the same time it offered excitement and countless opportunities for me. I thought about the words in my purpose statement: "Live without regrets and excuses." If I didn't have the courage to pursue what I had always wanted to do, would I look back one day and regret it? For me, the decision became very clear; I needed to head to Opportunityville. I called the firm and declined their job offer. I told my out-placement counselor that I had decided to start my own consulting firm. That was my last session at outplacement. There was to be no looking back, no turning left or right. I was headed to Opportunityville. As a reminder of my decision that day, I ordered a dog-tag necklace to wear around my neck each day. I had the letters LWRAELWPAP engraved on it, reminding me: Live Without Regrets And Excuses. Live With Passion and Purpose.

In one of the last conversations I had with by boss, Dan,

before leaving El Paso, I told him that whatever the future held for me, I hoped I could look back a year later and say that losing my job was the best thing that could have happened to me. One year later, I can say that in all honesty, I'm glad I lost my job. The last year of my journey has been one of the best of my life. I'm having a blast building my consultancy, and I enjoy the freedom it brings. It's been a lot of work, and I don't make anything close to the salary I made working for a large corporation. The nice annual bonus, stock options, and other perks are gone, but my quality of life is 100 percent better, and I'm doing what I love to do every day. My consulting practice is growing each month and expanding into new and exciting areas such as executive coaching. I can't imagine doing anything else.

I hope to see you in Opportunityville. Enjoy the journey, and live without regrets and excuses—live with passion and purpose!

Resources to Assist You in Your Career Transition

There are a number of excellent resources available to assist you in your job search. In this book, I discussed two excellent assessment instruments—the MBTI and the Strong Interest Inventory.

If you're interested in taking either or both of these assessments, please go to my Web site, www.davidjonesgroupllc.com, and look at my resource page.

My resource page also has two other tools to assist you in your job or career transition. You can download the following tools:

1. A template to assist you in preparing your household budget.
2. A template to track your networking activities.

I'd love to hear from you about how this book may have helped you in your transition. You can contact me at david@davidjonesgroupllc.com.

Example Values and Value Statements

Below are my thirteen values, value statements, and targeted actions. I find that my values haven't changed much over the last twenty years. Knowing my values helps simplify my life, and decision-making becomes much easier. For example, if my grown son calls me and asks me to do something with him one afternoon during a time I had planned on exercising, I have to make a decision between the two. Because my family is a more important value to me than my health, it's easy to decide to spend the time with my son. We might even decide to spend part of our time together exercising, which allows me to do two things I value at once.

Spiritual

I feel love, joy, peace, patience, kindness, goodness, faithfulness, gentleness, and self-control, because I honor God, because God knows me through my personal relationship with Jesus, and because God's Spirit lives in me and controls every aspect of my life.

Actions:

1. Daily prayer and Bible study
2. Attend Sunday School and church weekly
3. Read four Christian books yearly

Family

I feel happy and blessed, because I am the father of two fantastic kids and a husband to a wonderful wife whom I love unconditionally.

Actions:

1. Go on a date with Tanya weekly
2. Call my kids at least twice weekly
3. Call Dad twice weekly
4. Encourage and support my family
5. Take a vacation with Tanya each year
6. Do something with the kids each week if possible

Health

I feel healthy and strong, because I am in good physical condition, fuel my body with only high-energy foods, and exercise regularly. My body is the temple of the Holy Spirit, and I treat it with respect. My fitness gives me an advantage over my competitors and allows me to enjoy life to the fullest.

Actions:

1. Eat healthy veggies, fruits, whole grains, nuts, and lean meats daily
2. Drink eight glasses of water daily
3. Exercise for cardio four times each week
4. Exercise for strength three times each week
5. Vary my routine to avoid burnout

Friends

I feel fortunate and blessed, because I have many friends who care about me and enjoy my companionship. I will protect and grow these important relationships.

Actions:

1. Pray for my friends
2. Breakfast with JBC at least bimonthly
3. Do something with at least one of my friends each month

Attitude

I feel positive and optimistic, because daily I choose a can-do, positive approach to life. Attitude is a choice I make daily.

Actions:

1. Think positively in all circumstances
2. Read something positive daily
3. Control my feelings through my thoughts
4. Enjoy and be in each moment

Financial

I feel financially blessed, because I have sound investments that are growing, and I make wise financial decisions.

Actions:

1. Become debt-free
2. Don't spend more than I make
3. Give a tithe or 10 percent of my income to charitable causes
4. Invest for the future

Career

I feel excited and optimistic, because I am a successful business consultant, coach, author, and speaker who helps people and companies improve their performances and reach their potential.

Actions:

1. Keep my Web site updated
2. Spend 20 percent of my time on business development
3. Keep current on trends and news
4. Work hard and always be prepared

Priorities

I feel in control, focused, and targeted, because I have written goals, a daily plan based on "What's Important Now (WIN)," and continually think about the "next step."

Actions:

1. Do a weekly and daily written plan
2. Maintain a master to-do list that keeps my mind clear
3. Focus on what is important
4. Set goals

Thinking

I feel great, because I am thinking only about those things that move me toward my goals and dreams. My thoughts determine my attitude and control my feelings. I feed my mind with uplifting and motivating thoughts.

Actions:

1. Read Psalms and Proverbs daily
2. Ask myself if my thoughts are helping or hurting me throughout the day
3. Review my values and goals daily

Order

I feel organized, prepared, and in control, because I maintain order in my life and keep everything in its proper place.

Actions:

1. Allow fifteen minutes daily to organize
2. Keep a clean desk
3. Keep my filing up-to-date

Learning

I feel knowledgeable and wise, because I am continually learning and growing and challenging myself.

Actions:

1. Read a book each month
2. Read the newspaper daily
3. Read good blogs for ideas and thoughts
4. Don't be satisfied with the *status quo*
5. Ask each day, *What did I learn today?*

Thankfulness

I feel thankful and appreciative, because I am truly blessed by God in every area of my life. I rejoice in all things and daily count my blessings.

Actions:

1. Don't take anything for granted
2. Learn to be content

Excellence

Make excellence my signature in everything I do. Excellence will help ensure my success and will glorify my Lord.

Actions:

1. Do everything well

David Jones spent twenty-nine years working for one of the nation's largest energy companies. He worked in numer-

ous areas of the organization and in key management positions, including Director of Human Resources and Vice President of Eastern Operations. He left the company in 2007 as part of an asset disposition to another large energy company that did not retain his services, at which point David left to launch his own consulting/coaching company.

David Jones Group provides consulting, coaching, training, and speaking services to a wide variety of clients. The company's mission is to help organizations and leaders think bigger, perform better, and execute faster.

David holds a bachelor's degree from the University of Tennessee and a master's degree in business administration from the University of Houston. He and his wife, Tanya, reside in Franklin, Tennessee, where they participate in numerous business, church and charitable activities.

For information on David's consulting, coaching, training, speaking, and books, contact him at:

David F. Jones
www.davidjonesgroupllc.com
david@davidjonesgroupllc.com

REFERENCES

Part One

Colvin, Geoff. April 22, 2004. Long-term thinking. *Wall Street Week with Fortune*.

Frey, Rebecca L. Answers Corporation. *Encyclopedia of Medicine*. www.answers.com/topic/stress-top-ten-stressful-life-events

Part Two

Williams, Pat. 1995. *Go For The Magic*. Nashville: Thomas Nelson Publishers.

Maxwell, John. 2004. *Today Matters*. Nashville: Thomas Nelson and Time Warner Books.

Munroe, Myles. 1992. *In Pursuit of Purpose*, Shippensburg: Destiny Image.

Harkavy, Daniel. 2007. *Becoming A Coaching Leader*. Nashville: Thomas Nelson.

Morris, Betsy. 2003. Richard Branson: What a Life. *Fortune*.